MW01164887

How to Program Yourself for Success

This book is a jewel! It will revolutionize the way you think about what is possible in your life. Ben Hale is a master at how personal growth and professional advancement can be attained. I recommend this book as an important contribution to the psychology of self-programming for success.

Dr. Bill McDowell
Licensed Psychologist
Professor and Counseling Program Coordinator
Marshall University

Mr. Hale is to self-help and philosophy what Grandma Moses is to painting and art. Extraordinary and awe-inspiring! How fortunate we are that at the age of 95 Mr. Hale put pen to paper!

Eve M. Ellinger
Attorney and Counselor
Kegler, Brown, Hill & Ritter

Ben Hale's book is a tribute to the infinite capacity of the human mind to effect change. Thoreau in Walden states, "The masses...lead lives of quiet desperation. What is called resignation is confirmed desperation." Hale's book reveals the remedy! Each individual has the ability to achieve success by programming his mind to positive change. Consider the brain as hardware and the mind as software; we create our own software. Hale advises us to identify our talents, our abilities, and our interests; then set goals to move forward to the ideal life we have created in our minds. This is a "must read" for all who aspire to achieve the American Dream.

Dolores (Dee) Cook
Retired Teacher and Licensed Professional Career Counselor

How to Program Yourself for

Yourself for

Success

Ben Hale

HUMANOMICS
PUBLISHING

Systems where People Matter

A Grace Associates Book

ISBN 0-9746279-6-8
.

First Edition
Printed in the U.S.A.

Editorial Coordination: John Patrick Grace
    and Chris Washington
Cover Photo: Kris Clifford
Cover Design: Ariel McGill Price and Tabitha McCalop
Interior Design: Jennifer Adkins

Humanomics Publishing
945 Fourth Avenue, Suite 200A
Huntington, WV 25701
www.booksbygrace.com

Cover Photo: The Woodlands Retirement Community, main entry. Residence of Ben Hale, Huntington, WV.

To my posterity and all would-be achievers everywhere.
The vastness of your potential talents and abilities and
your desire to live better is a constant inspiration to me.

CONTENTS

Not enjoyment and not sorrow,
Is our destin'd end or way;
But to act, that each tomorrow
Find us farther than today.

In the world's broad field of battle,
In the bivouac of life,
Be not like dumb, driven cattle!
Be a hero in the strife!

Lives of great men all remind us
We can make our lives sublime,
And, departing, leave behind us
Footsteps on the sands of time.

Let us then be up and doing,
With a heart for any fate;
Still achieving, still pursuing,
Learn to labor and to wait.

from "A Psalm of Life"
Henry Wadsworth Longfellow

Preface

This book was written to suggest techniques and give examples of using your thinking to program yourself to be whatever you most want to be, to do all the things you most want to do, and to have all the things, conditions, and situations you most want in life. It was written also to convince you of the magnitude of the untapped potential powers and abilities you have within you at this very moment. From the first century AD to the present, students of human potential have expounded on the infinite powers of the human mind, concluding that the things we most want are not beyond us, that they are easily within our reach.

At a very early age I began to realize that I could, through my thinking, program myself to experience everything I most wanted in my life. At that point I did not think of it as programming, since "programming" was not a popular concept at that time.

Beginning at age twenty-one, with only six years of schooling, I programmed myself to accomplish things that for me were great and wonderful. I raised myself from a track laborer on a railroad to a successful salesman, and in the process I increased my income 600 percent the first month. From that job I went on to get a more sophisticated sales job with a 300 percent increase in income. After that point I programmed myself to begin a highly successful real estate brokerage business that I operated for twenty-five years. Following that I conducted real estate sales seminars. Many years after normal retirement age, because of my successes, I was called upon to teach in a community college. At the age of eighty-eight I programmed myself to conduct a weekly radio program, "The Old Philosopher."

The programming technique I used will work unfailingly for everyone. With it you are working with a law of nature that is as unfailing as the law of gravity. This book describes how average individuals have used this simple technique to program themselves to achieve greatness. The details of their journeys to greatness provide real-life examples of the universal application of this technique. Having the ability to program ourselves is by far our most precious heritage.

Our mind, in some ways, can be compared to a computer: what you put in is what you get out. The axiom "We become what we think" holds true. What you put in your mind is what comes out, and that is what determines your destiny.

There is widespread agreement amongst wise men of all ages that we actually become what we think. According to Proverbs 23:7, "As a man thinks in his heart, so is he." That being true, we are in complete control of our lives because we are privileged to have the ability to choose our every thought.

If you desire to be more, do more and have more, read this book often. Highlight or underline phrases that interest you. Write notes in the margin. Read it and reread it, analyze and reanalyze the message it contains. You will very soon be surprised and amazed at your achievements!

> Ben Hale
> Huntington, West Virginia
> February 2005

How to Program Yourself for

Success

Chapter 1:

*Programming Myself
for Success*

It is the heart that always sees before the head can see.

Thomas Carlyle

Everything of note that I ever did, I saw with my heart before I saw it with my head. That is to say, I always acted on hunches. When someone is fully programmed, powerful hunches come to their mind to direct their actions. It has been said that we have a little man sitting on our shoulder advising us. He tells us when to act and when to refrain from acting, and if we take his advice, we will never make a mistake.

I have found this concept to be true. More than once, I have taken giant steps on nothing but a hunch. Reason would have said not to take this step. Had my hunch been wrong, taking that step would have caused a financial catastrophe. It could have had a disastrous effect on my family. I would have been without work, without an income, with nothing whatsoever to sustain my family and me.

The little man on my shoulder said, "Go." And I acted. I did not take a chance. I did not put my family or myself into jeopardy. I loved my family too much to have taken that kind of risk. As I've discovered, though, when you become programmed, there is no risk.

I always acted with perfect confidence when I acted on a hunch. During the Great Depression of the 1930s, when 25.2 percent of the American work force was unemployed, because of the way I had programmed myself, I was able to leave a secure job on a railroad and take a job as a salesman. I did this despite the fact that I was terribly shy, had never sold anything in my life, and had to succeed at my new job in order to have any kind of an income. The little man on my shoulder, my hunch, said, "Go." I took his advice. I acted without fear or concern. I was totally positive that I would do well. And I did exceedingly well. I immediately increased my income 600%. I also found my rightful place in life. When one is properly programmed and acts on a hunch, the thing he is striving for always works out better than he had expected.

Although I did well as a salesman and dearly loved what I was doing, I left that job in a short time. I needed a car to deliver the merchandise I sold and had been borrowing one. With two months' worth of my earnings I could have bought a new car. It never once occurred to me to buy one. I had never owned a car and simply could not see myself owning one. The fact is, I was not programmed to own a car. I therefore gave up a job I loved.

Six years later I was working at a job I did not like. I was a meat cutter in a coal company store. As time passed, my dislike for that work became more intense. I concluded that in order to be happy and enjoy life I would have to leave the store and get back into the work I loved, which was being a salesman.

I did not know of anything I could do to cause this to happen. I was working ten to twelve hours a day, six days a week. I did not have time to look for another job.

I continued to think, to search my brain for something I could do to bring it about. Goethe, the great German poet, said, "When one makes a commitment, Providence moves too." When one is programmed to achieve a certain thing, he makes a commitment. I had made a commitment to get a new job, and Providence really moved.

The company for which I was working gave each store manager and each department manager a copy of Dale Carnegie's book *How to Win Friends and Influence People* and insisted they read it. I was manager of my department, therefore I was given a copy of the book. That book totally and completely changed my life forever. I spent many months reading and rereading it. I analyzed and reanalyzed what it was saying. I was intrigued by what it taught. I could hardly believe I was twenty-nine years old and was not already aware of the things that book was teaching me. I began to apply some of the principles it set forth and was amazed at how effective those principles were in affecting the thoughts and actions of others.

Despite the fact that 17.9 percent of all Americans were unemployed, I was convinced I could use the principles I had found in the book to get a better job. Whereupon, I told my wife I was going to quit my job. She asked me what I was going to do. I told her I was going to use the principles I had found in the book to get a better job and that I was going to use those same principles to make the job pay. That is exactly what I did.

When I quit the job, we lived in a house owned by the company for which I worked. When an employee left the company's employ he was expected to vacate their property. We had no house to which we could move, no job to which I could go and no money to last us more than about a week.

By quitting that job, however, I did not put my family or myself in jeopardy. Carnegie's *How to Win Friends and Influence People* had helped me to program myself to the extent that I was absolutely sure things would work out. The morning after I quit my job I was out walking, enjoying some fresh air and sunshine, when I came upon the superintendent of the mine. He asked me what I was going to do. I told him I was going to rest for a couple of days and then was going to work somewhere. He said, "You should get a job selling automobiles." That was far, far beyond anything for which I felt capable. If he had said, "You should run for governor," I would not have been more surprised. Then he asked me if I wanted to go to work for him.

I went to work for him the next day as a

laborer doing all sorts of odd jobs. In a few weeks a man I was working with asked me if I had seen the new 1940 model Chevrolet. He told me it was the most beautiful thing he had ever laid his eyes on. I knew right then that I had found the solution to my problem. I knew I had found the selling job I wanted. That evening I went to town to see if I could find one of those beautiful cars. I found one and it was indeed beautiful. It was what was called a two-tone. The color of the lower part was something near an orange color. The upper part was a cream color or beige.

The next day I was an automobile salesman. When the local Chevrolet dealership opened for business that morning, I was there. I used a technique found in Carnegie's book in applying for the job and was hired. I knew nothing about selling automobiles. Despite my lack of experience I was so thoroughly programmed I was sure I would do well. I sold a car the first day I worked there. I earned more money that day than I had ever earned before in one day in my life.

There were twelve salesmen working there. I made thirteen. They were all experienced salesmen, yet right from the beginning I was second in sales. That is to say, only one of the thirteen salesmen sold more cars than I did. This did not happen because I was intelligent, knowledgeable or knew how to sell. It happened only because I was programmed.

I was working there when World War II became really intense in Europe. The only reason I stopped was because of the war. American companies had discontinued manufacturing cars for domestic use; therefore we had no cars to sell. I was out of a job.

I will cite a number of examples in a single story of my heart knowing before my head knew. My family and I had left Logan, West Virginia, where I had done exceedingly well in the real estate business, and had moved to Huntington, West Virginia. I had not planned to get involved in that business in our new location. I had something else I wanted to do, which was to teach selling and do motivational speaking. I wanted to get a job selling for a company doing business nationwide. My plan was to work hard and move up in the company. That did not work out. I had not programmed myself for that and had not acted on a hunch. I acted on reason, which many times cannot be trusted. I worked a short time for several different companies. In every job I was either not happy with a company's method of operation, was not sufficiently sold on the product, or did not feel comfortable working for the person that would be my immediate supervisor. As soon as I became aware of one of these situations I would resign.

I continued that until I was so broke I pawned a shotgun for $57.00 to buy food for my family, which consisted of a wife and six school-age children. Although we were on the verge of being without some of our everyday needs, neither my family nor I were ever deprived of sufficient food, clothing or any of the necessities of life.

I then had a little conference with myself. I did what everyone should do more often. *I sat and listened to my heart.* It became abundantly clear to me that I should get back into the real estate business. My thinking was that since I had no money, there was no way I could do so at that point. But I had a hunch I would find a way very soon.

That day Sears Roebuck and Company (now Sears) was advertising for a salesman. I applied for the job. I filled out an application form and handed it to the man in charge. He looked at it and said, "We will call you in a day or two." I told him there would be no need to call. He said, "Why not?" I told him I was going to work somewhere that day. This must have impressed him because he replied, "I like your attitude. You're hired."

I still did not know what I would be selling. As it turned out it was something *I* was truly sold on, encyclopedias and a set of books for children. They were sold together or separately.

I would be working with a small crew of men that traveled from city to city. In each city the company would rent an apartment and have six or eight telephones installed. We lived and made phone calls there.

The company furnished 3-by-5 cards with names, addresses and phone numbers. The cards were arranged according to the street numbers so all our appointments would be in the same general area. Each of us was to make calls every day until we had at least six appointments. When we worked a city out we immediately moved on to another city.

I was hired on a Monday morning. The manager told me I would be paid $50.00 the first week while I was in training. I knew full well there was no way I could take care of my family and myself for a week with only $50.00. I knew—that is, *my heart knew* beyond any shadow of a doubt I would find a way to earn more. *I had not a thing to go on but a hunch.* It said, "Go." *As always, my heart was right.*

We had a sales presentation three legal-size pages long, which we were to memorize before we went out to sell. A few minutes after I was hired, the manager directed me to a city eighty miles away where they had set up and a crew of men had been working. I got there about noon. I studied the sales presentation that afternoon and all day the next day.

The following morning I told the manager I wanted to go out that day. He said, "There's no way you can do that. You don't know the sales presentation." I had come up with an idea, a hunch I was sure would work. I said, "Leave that to me." He said, "Get on the phone and get some appointments."

We used a memorized telephone pitch, "Good morning Mrs. Brown, my name is Ben Hale. I'm with Sears Roebuck and company. Sears Roebuck is going to place a limited number of reference libraries in homes in this area. It's the one given away on the house party program on television. Is this something you feel you would like to have in your home?" I got my six appointments with little difficulty.

My first appointment was four o'clock that afternoon with a young couple that had two or three children between the ages of about four and ten. Their home was a lovely, nicely decorated, two-story house. I noticed they had several books. That was always a good sign. The more books people owned, the more likely they were to buy.

The idea I had come up with was to read the sales presentation to the prospective buyers. Once I met this couple and got through the preliminaries, I said to the Browns, "What I am going to show you is relatively new to Sears Roebuck and it's brand new to me. I have a three-page written sales presentation. I am supposed to have it memorized, but I don't. Is it all right if I just read it to you?" They both said, "Yes." I had worked a day and a half on memorizing it and therefore I could read it fairly well.

When a customer knows a salesman is coming they build up an unconscious resistance to them. Because I didn't know the sales presentation they assumed I wasn't a good salesman, or, in fact, any kind of salesman at all. By admitting I did not know the presentation I destroyed their resistance to me. This led them to trust me as a person and to trust the presentation and the product I was selling.

When I finished reading the presentation they both wanted the books. They not only bought the encyclopedia, they also bought the children's books. My commission on that sale was $120.00. When it was over Mr. Brown shook my hand and said, "You are the best salesman I have ever seen." My feelings were that the Browns had done a wonderful thing for themselves and their family. They were happy with their purchase. I felt that I had done a wonderful thing for the Browns.

I enjoyed making the sale more than I enjoyed

earning the money. My total earnings for the week were $309.00. With inflation that would be more than $5,000.00 today. I continued selling books until I achieved the goal I was attempting to program myself to achieve, which was to get back into the real estate business. However, I did not think of things in those terms simply because programming was pretty much unheard of back then. That was decades before computers and talk of programming became popular.

I mentioned I would cite in a single story several examples of the heart knowing before the head knew. I had read a great book a few years earlier, *The Magic of Believing*, by Claude M. Bristol. In that book Bristol suggested that we talk aloud to ourselves when we have a goal. We should tell ourselves that we will achieve our goal.

As I drove from appointment to appointment and back and forth from home on the weekends, I talked aloud to myself almost constantly. I told myself thousands and thousands of times, "I know there is a way for me to get back in the real estate business, and I know I will find it." This continued for about six months.

On a Monday morning I went out of town to work. For that week I would be the only member of the crew working in that city. As I entered my hotel room, just as I passed through the doorway, because of the way the positive self-talk had programmed me, an incredible idea came to my mind.

The idea was how I could start a real estate business with the money I had in my pocket, a sum less than one hundred dollars.

Starting a real estate business with that amount of money would appear to be not only impossible, but also unthinkable. Who would think of such a thing? I certainly wouldn't have thought of it had I not been so thoroughly programmed. Because I was so well programmed, my heart could see it clearly.

The little man on my shoulder reminded me of things I had learned while in the business in Logan. I was reminded that I could knock on doors and find people that would let me have their house to sell. I had done that the first day I worked in the business in Logan.

The newspaper would allow me to advertise

in it and would not expect payment until the first of the next month. I knew—*that is, my heart knew that when the time came to pay, I would have the money.* I could write advertisements that would attract "ready-to-buy-now buyers." I could handle those calls in a way that would result in sales.

I immediately returned home. My wife asked, "What are you doing back home?" because she knew we needed money to be able to eat every day. I told her I was going back into the real estate business. She said, "How?" She knew we had no money, no income, no net worth and therefore no borrowing power. I told her I didn't know yet.

Again, I did not put my family in jeopardy. I was totally confident I would succeed. I had a hunch to visit a friend that was in the business. I had no reason to go except that my hunch said to go. While I was there another real estate broker came in. He had a place for rent that was closer to town and asked my friend if he was interested. My friend told him he was not interested in moving.

I had not intended to have an office in the beginning. I knew I would have to have some furniture and did not have money to buy it. I was going to work out of my home until I got the business going. However, I thought it would be interesting to know what he had to offer. I asked him a couple of questions about it. He asked me if I was interested in it. I told him I did not know but would like to see it anyway. Not only was the place he showed me a good location for a real estate office, an adequate amount of office furniture was included in the lease.

When one is well programmed and acts on a hunch, things always seem to work out better than had been anticipated.

He said, "The rent is $100.00 a month, payable in advance." I would be required to take a three-year lease. There was no way I could pay that amount. I simply did not have the money.

I did something I had never done before and have never done since. I had always carried my paper money in my billfold. That day I had two twenty-dollar bills in my front pants pocket. When he told me what the rent would be I immediately, without thinking, handed him the two twenties and told him I would take it but was only going to pay forty dollars a month. He accepted the money.

Three days later I was open for business. The first morning I started knocking on doors a short distance from the office. The third door I knocked on I got a house for sale. I immediately placed an advertisement for it in the local paper. When the paper came out the following morning the friend I had visited called. He said that he had a couple looking for a house similar to the one I had advertised. He wanted to know if he could show it. He sold it that day. Because there was a loan on it that could be assumed, it could be closed in a couple of days. I sold another small house that month. That gave me an income of $412.50 for the month. That was not a bad monthly income in 1954.

The business prospered from the beginning. I always had an adequate supply of properties to sell. Within three to four months I owned a half interest in a subdivision worth many thousands of dollars in which I had made no investment. Before I had sold all those lots, I owned a half interest in another valuable subdivision that had not cost me one cent. I owned interests in two other subdivisions. I also developed two subdivisions for other people. Because of my programming I had lots of good things happen to me. I built, on speculation, more than one hundred houses. And I conducted more than one hundred real estate sales seminars in a five-state area.

When one is sufficiently programmed and the heart sees and the little man on your shoulder says "go" you positively will not fail. What's more, when one acts on a hunch one always has perfect confidence, and there is never any fear or concern.

Deep within your consciousness is the realization that your life has a purpose, a destiny, a meaning that must be discovered. Until this is achieved you will experience boredom, dissatisfaction, frustration, the feeling of hunger or despair. To be working for a great purpose larger than yourself is one of the secrets of making life thrilling and exciting.

Harry Emerson Fosdick

Everyone is entitled to a thrilling, exciting life, and everyone can have such a life. There is never a reason for anyone to be bored, lonely, or experience feelings of desperation. Euripedes, a famous Greek playwright who lived around 400 B.C., said, "Each person is born with a special excellence." Discovering that special excellence and using it to serve others will result in a life filled with satisfaction and excitement. There will be no time for boredom or loneliness.

One of the greatest and most important discoveries one can ever make is to find that *special excellence* Euripedes mentioned. James Russell Lowell, a great American poet, said, "No man was ever born whose work was not born with him." Until one finds that special excellence, the work he was born to do which is his rightful place in life, he cannot experience a full measure of success and happiness.

It has been estimated that only a small percentage of people, about one in twenty, actually find the place they were born to fill. Failing to find yourself will deprive you of the success and happiness you are entitled to and could have had. Instead, you are likely to spend your years working at something you would rather not be doing. Most, if not all, of your days will be spent watching a clock, looking forward with anxiety to quitting time, vacation, and retirement.

Doing the thing you were born to do is so tremendously important; you should search and never give up searching until you find it. Robert Herrick, an English poet, said, "Attempt the end and never stand in doubt; nothing is so hard but search will find it out."

One way to discover your purpose in life, the work you were born to do, is to decide what is the most important change you would most like to see take place in your life, your circumstances right now. It could be a small thing: a dependable car, a job, a more pleasant job, or a new wardrobe. It could be anything.

Make an exhaustive list of the important changes you would like to have happen in your life as of now. Come up with as many as you can. Try to come up with a dozen or more. Take your time. Study the list. Give each thing you have listed careful thought. Now select the five changes you would most like to see take place immediately. After careful deliberation select the one change that is most important to you.

Whatever it is, you can program yourself to make it happen. Write it down. Put it where you will see it often. Better still, write it on a small card and have it laminated. Carry it in your pocket or purse. Talk aloud to yourself. Tell yourself repeatedly, "I know there is a way for me to achieve my goal, and I know I will find it." Over a period of days, weeks, or even months you may tell yourself this thousands of times. Picture in your mind repeatedly how things will be once you achieve your goal. Upon achieving this goal you will see another goal, a bigger and better goal. You will continue to see bigger, better and more important goals. Following this method always brings success. There is no way it can fail. It is a law of nature that is as dependable as the law of gravity.

A word of caution: never divulge your goal to anyone unless it is to some close friend that will understand. To talk about it may give you a small degree of the same satisfaction you would experience by achieving the goal. This could take the sharp edge off of your desire to achieve the goal, thus weakening your efforts.

If thou canst plan a noble deed,
And never flag till it succeed.
Though in the strife thy heart should bleed,
Whatever obstacles control,
Thine hour will come – go on true soul!
Thou'll win the prize, thou'lt reach the goal.

Clarence Mackay

As I mentioned earlier, when I was a very young man I sold Chevrolet automobiles for about two years. During the first month I worked there, all the Chevrolet salesmen in the region were required to attend a big sales training and motivational rally. I heard an outstanding speech that day. It was given by a moving speaker we will call John Miller.

When Miller finished his speech I had a new goal. *I had planned a noble deed.* I wanted to do what John Miller was doing. My plan of action was to work hard and sell so many cars I would attract the attention of the people running the Chevrolet Division of General Motors. I was hoping they would want me to do something similar to what Miller was doing. That plan did not work out. Because of World War II, General Motors discontinued manufacturing cars for domestic use. They converted all their efforts to manufacture war materials only. I was out of a job. I did not achieve my goal. Neither did I abandon it. *I did not flag.* My desire to do what I had seen and heard John Miller do was very strong. That desire was to teach selling and do motivational speaking.

Many years later when I was in the real estate business, I closed the business when it was at its peak. Thinking it would open doors for me to teach selling and do motivational speaking, I joined Success Motivation Institute of Waco, Texas. They were selling motivational and sales training records. I did exceedingly well with them until I questioned some of the methods they used to market their product. I then joined the Nightingale Conant company of Chicago. They were selling pretty much the same type of products as the company I had just left.

Most of the Nightingale Conant products were programs recorded by Nightingale and they were superb. I believed so strongly in them I must have shown a lot of enthusiasm when I presented them. Several of the companies I called on wanted to hire me to sell for them. The owner of one of the largest real estate companies in the city wanted to hire me as his sales manager. I told him I was not interested. He did not take that lightly. He then asked me to be his sales manager for six months only. When I told him I was not at all interested in being a sales manager, he said, "I have got to have some of that stuff." I assumed he was talking about my enthusiasm. "Could I get you to do some sales training for me?" I told him that might be a possibility. He then asked me what I would charge to conduct ten two-hour sessions. We never settled on a price, but he paid me very well. When I finished the ten, he wanted me to do ten more immediately, which I agreed to do. After that he had me come back several times and do two-hour sessions.

He and I attended a real estate sales seminar. The conductor of that seminar was the best I had ever heard, and I had attended many of them. When it was over he said, "Ben, you are twice as good as that fellow." I decided if I was that good I was going to go into the seminar business.

I began at once to program myself to make it happen. Knowing how powerful it is to use pictures to remind oneself of one's goal, I put a huge picture of a large audience on the wall of my bathroom. Every time I entered that room I would stop and pretend to be speaking to that audience.

I ordered a book on how to conduct seminars, which I read and reread several times. It was loaded with information I needed about promoting and conducting seminars. I also pretended that I had already achieved my goal. Every time I got in my car to go anywhere, I pretended to be going somewhere to conduct a seminar, and every time I came home, when I got out of my car, I pretended to be getting home from conducting a seminar.

This very soon programmed me to the extent that I felt confident enough to go forward with my project. I arranged to hold the first one in the city in which I lived. I mailed a brochure to every real estate company in every city within fifty miles. The response was better than I had expected. That was a half-day seminar. The registration fee was $25.00 and included lunch. That first seminar was so successful I decided to expand.

I mailed out 16,000 brochures, one to each real estate broker in North Carolina, South Carolina, and Georgia. I was to conduct two seminars, one in Raleigh, North Carolina and the other one in

Atlanta, Georgia. Because of the way I had pro-grammed myself, they were both huge successes.

I then made a terrible mistake. I got big dollar signs in my eyes. I acted against my own better judgment. I listened to reason, instead of listening to my heart. Reason said, "You will make big bucks." The great British playwright George Bernard Shaw said, "The man who listens to reason is lost." I had 35,000 brochures printed. I mailed one to every real estate company in Ohio, Michigan, Indiana, Wisconsin and part of Illinois.

I was to conduct a single seminar in each of those states. To my dismay, I got not one reply. The brochures named the cities in which the seminars were to be held, but did not have the dates they were to be held. I had spent a ton of money having the printing done, getting the brochures ready to mail, and posting them, all to no avail.

I listened to reason and lost. I was so low on money I could not continue. *Again, however, I did not flag.*

In a short time I began conducting seminars on a much smaller scale. I would go to a city and call on realty companies to promote a series, usually five two-hour seminars, to be held from ten o'clock AM until noon. I would go to a nearby city and promote one to be held from two PM until four PM. I would promote another one in another nearby city to be conducted in the evening. These were all to be on the same day over a five-week period.

I did that until I reached the age well past what most would consider retirement age. Shortly after I stopped having the seminars, I got a call from a university wanting to know whether I would be interested in teaching a course in real estate in their community college. I worked there about a year. They never got around to offering a course in real estate; however, I taught several courses on how to be a successful salesperson.

The university was in a city where many people were on welfare. The state had given the school a grant to train people to try to help them become more employable. They were taught how to do resumes, how to handle interviews, and other things one needs to know about how to get a job.

I had the classes in the evenings. My job was

to convince the students they could do it. These people were so interesting that working with them provided lots of fun and excitement. I loved it. I might add that a little more than 70 percent of them got good-paying jobs. Some of them got jobs and left before the course ended. Most of them got what they wanted. I got what I wanted. We all had a ball.

Don't flag. Thine hour will come. Thou'lt win the prize, thou'lt reach the goal.

Opportunities are out there for you to be anything you want to be.

Colin Powell

There is no shortage of opportunity. It abounds on every hand. It is constantly knocking on your heart's door. In his poem "Opportunity," Ralph Malone allows her to speak:

They do me wrong who say I come no more
When once I knock and fail to find you in,
For every day I stand outside your door
To bid you wake, and rise to fight and win.

There is no way you could want to be something, even something great, if you did not have the innate ability to bring it into being. The power that lets you have the desire is the same power that gives you the ability to get it. One good idea could change you from what you are to what you would most like to be. And there are no shortages of great ideas. Thomas A. Edison, the most prolific inventor of all time, when asked where he got the ideas for all his wonderful inventions, replied, "From the ether." There are ideas out there in countless numbers just waiting for you to seize upon them. You need only engage yourself in searching. Then the idea you need will appear in your mind.

Barney was an average young man whom I knew very well. He had a young family and was working for a very low wage. He was not satisfied with the lifestyle he was providing for his family. He wanted to do more. The possibility of that did not look promising. He had only a half dozen years of schooling and had learned no trade that could provide high wages.

What this man finally accomplished seemed totally impossible at the time. He proved over and over that there is no shortage of opportunity or ideas that can change one's life. He was undoubtedly searching when what turned out to be a life-changing idea came to his mind. The idea was to go into the trucking business in a way small enough that he could operate it in the evenings after his eight hours of work and on weekends. Despite his low wages, Barney was able to buy a very old and very used truck.

Being prompt and serving his customers well, his business grew quickly. As his business increased he acquired bigger and better trucks.

Along with his trucking business he acquired a bulldozer and began an excavation business. That business prospered so much that he gave up the trucking business and concentrated his efforts on his new earthmoving business. Over the years his excavating business grew to the point where he had many huge earthmoving machines, dump trucks, bulldozers, huge gasoline shovels, and every other kind of machinery used in that business. Barney's company was for years the biggest company of its kind for miles around.

All this was just the beginning of the things Barney accomplished. He eventually owned several very prosperous businesses. He acquired land that he subdivided and sold building lots. Last but certainly not least, he owned a coal mine, which, in all probability, was his most profitable business venture. Most of these businesses were managed either by him, or by one of his sons or grandsons.

Barney not only did well financially, he also had a great life. He had a wonderful, close-knit family that lived well and enjoyed life. Perhaps Barney's greatest accomplishment, the thing that brought him the most happiness, was that his success did not change his demeanor. He was always just Barney.

You have all of the qualities necessary to have as great a life as Barney had. You need only settle on the thing you most want to do and program yourself to bring that thing into being.

Benjamin Disraeli, former Prime Minister of England, offered some great advice for anyone that wants to be more: "Nurture your mind with great thoughts. Just one thought, just one ray of light, can energize and change an individual's abilities and existence. Great men and great deeds are the results of great thoughts." The fact that imagination is the pristine power of the human mind has long been recognized by the greatest thinkers.

Dr. Alex Osborne

Many great thinkers have had something to say about the power of the imagination. Henry David Thoreau said, "I learned this, at least, by my experiment: that if one advances confidently in the direction of his dream, and endeavors to live the life which he has imagined, he will meet with a success unexpected in common hours."

It seems that the imagination is pure power. Norman Vincent Peale, who for fifty years was one of America's most popular and best-loved clergymen, had this to say about it: "Imaging, the forming of mental pictures or images, is based on the principle that there is a deep tendency in human nature to ultimately become precisely like that which we imagine ourselves as being."

Jonathan Edwards, considered one of the most brilliant theological minds ever produced in North America, said, "The ideas and images in men's minds are the invisible power that constantly governs them." Even the Bible has something to say about the awesome power of the imagination in Proverbs 29:18: "Where there is no vision the people perish."

If you cannot get a vision of yourself doing a thing, it is impossible for you to do it. Conversely, you can be, do, or have anything or any set of circumstances you want, no matter how great they are. If you persist in imagining yourself as having it, the power of your imagination will program you in such a way that you will find a way to bring it about.

Imagination and self-image are basically the same thing. Education usually enhances these, but not always. There are many highly intelligent individuals with college degrees who toil at the bottom of the ladder. All those years of schooling usually program one for success. Yet some people graduate and are still not able to imagine themselves as successful. There are also many individuals with little or no formal education that have been able to do the thing that always brings success. Some of them have accumulated vast fortunes. Some have served as heads of states. At least one U.S. president, Andrew Johnson, never went to school. He surely must have been a great dreamer.

According to the wise men quoted above, the imagination is capable of bringing our thoughts into physical form. Based on what they have said, when one has a goal, no matter how impossible it appears to be, in order to achieve it, the only thing one needs to do to bring it into being is to form a mental picture of how things will be when the goal is achieved and impress it upon one's subconscious mind. That is, program yourself to bring it into being.

Most writers that have written about what one needs to do in order to use more of his potential name a great list of things one must do in order to bring it about. The many things these writers say one has to do actually work. The reason they work is that they help to program the person who's doing them. *I have said this before and I will say it again: the only thing you need to do to achieve any goal is to program yourself by impressing it upon your subconscious mind..*

Dr. James N. Farr, in his great book *Supraconscious Leadership*, said, "We cannot have an experience for which we do not have in our mind a program that transmits our energy to create it."

PROGRAM YOURSELF FOR SUCCESS

Our only limitations are not programming bigger and better things for ourselves by not imagining bigger and better things for ourselves. Our imagination sets the limits of our accomplishments.

There is a key to achievement that will open any door, meet any challenge, overcome any obstacle, achieve any goal, and bring you all the things you most want from life. That key is your thinking.

Chapter 2:

The Power of the Mind

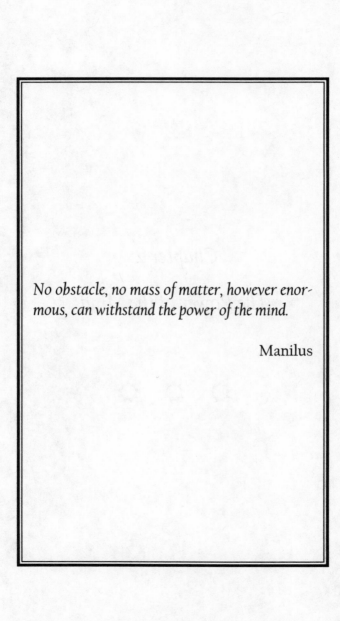

No obstacle, no mass of matter, however enor-mous, can withstand the power of the mind.

Manilus

It would be wonderful to have a magic wand that you could wave and get the things, conditions, and circumstances you most want in life. You do not have such a wand, of course; there is no such thing. However, you do have within you at this very moment an unlimited creative force that can and will bring you all the things you most desire if your thinking is right.

The late Earl Nightingale, who was a nationally famous actor, lecturer and writer, made a fabulous discovery. According to his own story he, along with his family, lived on the West Coast near a marina. He saw people who owned huge yachts come and go in fine automobiles. He thought the people who were doing so well knew some secret and anyone who was aware of it could become very wealthy.

He was right! There is such a secret! However, it is a secret only to those who do not know about it. In search of that secret, beginning at age thirteen, he read every book in the local library on philosophy. He began a search that lasted seventeen years and finally discovered the secret.

Once he felt confident that he was aware of the secret, he announced that within five years he would be a millionaire. And he was! He made a record explaining that important secret. Having become the best-selling talk record ever produced, in five years it made him a millionaire. What Nightingale discovered has been called "the secret of the ages" and has also been called "the strangest secret in the world." It is not a secret at all, but it is the simple concept that *we actually do become what we think.*

The fact that you are reading this indicates that you, like Nightingale and almost everyone else, would like to be more, do more, and have more. Deep down inside you there is a feeling that you can do better, that you can grow, that you can be somebody, that you have what it takes to really go, if only you could just get started. That feeling is there because you have enormous untapped potential lying dormant within you right now. The unused potential, power, and ability you have are what you must bring out to accomplish what you most want. You have all the creative ability and all the mental and physical attributes you could possibly need to take you as high and as far as you wish to go. You, like all human beings, have the power to create your own successful life.

No estimate is more in danger of erroneous calculations than those by which one computes the force of his or her own genius.

Samuel Johnson

In the book *The New Psychology of Persuasion and Motivation in Selling,* Robert Avery Whitney and others reported that A. Zalznik and his associates, doing research at Harvard University, came to the conclusion that "achievement, drive, or personal motivation does not need to be 'created' or 'instilled' into you from the outside. It is 'there.' It only needs to be released, given an opportunity to express itself, and perhaps to be stimulated." By using your limitless power, mental resources, and motivation, you are capable of achieving more in a few years than the average person achieves in a lifetime.

The future holds a lot for you because with your unlimited talents and abilities, and your motivation, you hold a lot for the future. The fact that you have all this untapped potential and all these unlimited talents and abilities lying dormant within you should bring to your mind some of the most important questions of your life. How can I awaken the giant that sleeps within me? How can I use the unlimited powers and abilities that I have? How can I get maximum results?

The wonderful news is that you *can*, and you can achieve greatly. Nothing can stop you. There is nothing holding you back or restraining you in any way. Anything that appears to be a barrier is only a figment of your imagination. You are free, completely free, to go as high as you care to go.

The first step is to realize your dissatisfaction with your present circumstances. The more you dislike your current way of life, the more likely you are to do something about it. Harry Emerson Fosdick, a popular clergyman in New York for forty years, a college professor and writer of several books, said, "An antagonistic environment is often our very best friend." You must have desire, an all-consuming desire, to change your environment and your way of life. There would be no conscious will or motivation to do better if you were happy and satisfied with your present circumstances.

With that desire, you also must have hope. Samuel Johnson, an English lexicographer and poet, said, "Where there is no hope there can be no endeavor." You simply cannot strive for a thing or a situation unless you think it is possible for you to get it. Individuals without hope never advance. One without hope is at a terrible disadvantage; he never gets beyond an uninteresting, unproductive life of mediocrity. He never shines. If you do not have hope, it means you do not see any possible way to do better. It means you do not have belief in yourself. As long as you harbor such thoughts, you will not advance. You will never have an opportunity to use the enormous powers and abilities that were born with you.

If one is without hope, then one can make no effort to gain a better place in life. He is locked in his present unsatisfactory circumstances forever. One of the beautiful characteristics of nature is that hope can be gained or developed without effort. Sometimes a realization of this sort occurs when you see a friend accomplish a task you considered beyond his or her ability. You could come to the firm belief, "If he can do that, I can do it." When such a thing happens you will be transformed. You will be a changed person.

When someone is striving to achieve an important goal, an incident can take place that can give that person new hope that will immediately enable him to make a great forward leap.

When I first entered the real estate business, an hour before I made that move, I would have thought it was far beyond anything of which I was capable. As I mentioned earlier, I called a real estate company about a house they were advertising. The man that showed me the house was the most unpolished person I had ever seen in business. He was wearing what had perhaps once been a good suit and a white shirt and tie, neither of which fit well. He was driving a car that had obviously been in a fire and then painted a maroon color with a paintbrush. It appeared to have been reupholstered by a carpenter or a blacksmith.

I had dealt with the public enough that I knew how to get information from people. Because of this man's appearance and the car he was driving, I wanted to know whether he was successful. I learned that he was doing exceedingly well. My hopes skyrocketed. I thought, if this man can make a living doing this, I know I will get rich. That incident, I feel sure, had a lot to do with helping to program myself to do well in the business.

Without hope and without belief in yourself, you will never accomplish anything. But with hope and with belief in yourself, nothing you want is beyond you.

Only in proportion as we are desirous of living better do we live at all.

Jose y Ortega Gasset

There is no joy in the status quo. He who is willing to settle for things as they are has no life. Zestful living comes only with having a purpose. Striving to achieve some definite goal that originally would have seemed far beyond one's capabilities adds interest and excitement to one's life. There really is no status quo. We are either advancing or we are retrograding. Each of us has a hidden sense of urgency to grow.

There is no limit to how well we are capable of serving or how greatly we can succeed except for the limits we impose upon ourselves. To discover and use your natural talents and abilities could bring you great fame, great happiness, and great psychological fulfillment. You may discover the work you were born to do by being unwilling to settle for things as they are.

An article in my local newspaper written by a college professor said that everyone reaches a point where a profound question should be asked: "Is there life before death?" The true answer is, "Only if there is purpose."

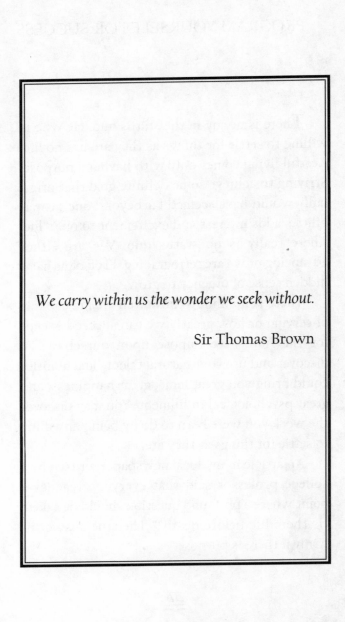

We carry within us the wonder we seek without.

Sir Thomas Brown

Each of us carries within us incredible wonder. In some instances it is the type of wonder that can make one rich and famous. Our minds are capable of things *light years* beyond our ability to comprehend. Sparks of creative genius constantly flit about in our minds. It is up to us to seize those sparks and fan them into a full blaze. It could be a new, ingenious way to transport people. It could be the business you are thinking about going into. You may feel that you would like to try your hand at producing beautiful artwork. These are divine inspirations, things that you were born to do.

But your reasoning says, "No, don't do that. It's too dangerous. You could lose your shirt." These ideas may appear to be things beyond your capabilities. Some individuals, although they are immeasurably capable of doing the thing they feel they would like to do, put it off for years. They surely would have had a better, more productive life had they acted when the idea first occurred to them.

If you take one step toward accomplishing one

of these ideas, you will see another step, and then another step and still another. This will continue until you are well on your way to a successful career. Remember the Chinese proverb, "A journey of a thousand miles begins with a single step."

Grandma Moses (Anna Mary Robertson Moses) was born in 1860 and lived to be 101 years old. She was a famous self-trained American painter who lived the busy life of a farm wife. She always felt that she could paint and that she would like to try it. However, she was so busy she just did not have any time for painting until her late seventies, when she could no longer do the hard farm work. At that time she completed her first painting.

Most of her paintings were scenes of the farm life she knew so well. Her paintings very soon become enormously popular. Her painting *Thanksgiving Turkey* is in the Metropolitan Museum of Art in New York City. At the age of 100 she illustrated "'Twas the Night before Christmas." She is named in the list of Women Who Left Their Stamps on History. She would never have had thoughts of becoming a painter, though, had she not possessed the mental capacity to be an artist.

Being in the real estate business, I was familiar with the story of the life of an older man who was in the business at the same time I was. He had within him a wonder, a hidden skill, or, one could say, a special talent that would have given him a happy, successful and prosperous life-long career in a business he loved.

He knew all his life that he would like to be in the real estate business. But he neglected the wonder he had within him and went outside of his aptitude, outside of himself and into a career that must have been to him, to some degree, drudgery. It was a life sentence of many long days of watching a clock, anxiously looking forward to quitting time, payday, and retirement. Once he had served his life sentence and reached the age when he could retire, he decided to go for his dream, the wonder that had been within him from the beginning.

Along with a partner, he started a real estate brokerage business, which, from day one, proved highly successful and very rewarding. He remained in the business until he became quite wealthy and until his age demanded he give up the work he so thoroughly enjoyed.

These inspirations may flash into your mind at any age. However, acting on an inspiration that flashes into your mind at an early age could mean the difference between a full, happy, productive life and a dull, uneventful life. The choice is entirely up to you.

We have everything we need in life to accomplish everything we dare to dream.

Guy Findley

"If you can dream it, you can do it" is an often-heard cliché, but it is nevertheless true. You do not lack the strength. You lack the initiative to go for it. Most of the great students of human potential have agreed that we have no limits except the ones we impose upon ourselves. The same power that lets you have the dream is the power that brings it into being. Therefore you would not have the dream if you did not have all the equipment necessary to make it become a reality in your life.

Wilson wasn't the brightest boy that ever lived, yet genius sparked in even his imagination. When we were boys, there was an old automobile frame sitting next to a vacant lot where we played ball. The old frame still had a gasoline tank, which was originally under the front seat where most gasoline tanks were placed then. It also still had a steering wheel and a gearshift lever.

When Wilson was well into his teen years he would sit on the gas tank of the old car pretending to drive it, with one hand turning the steering wheel and the other hand on the gear shift knob, moving it continually forward and backward as if he were shifting gears. While steering the car and shifting gears he would continue repeating for a great length of time, "High low gear, high low gear."

While our imaginary chauffeur may have done some out-of-the-ordinary things, he also dared to dream. Not too many moons after sitting on the gasoline tank shifting gears, he joined the Army just before the beginning of World War II. While he was still a buck private in the Army, sparks of genius came to his mind. In his imagination he could see a better sight for a machine gun than the one the Army used. He did something about it.

According to his family he invented a better sight for machine guns, which was immediately put into use by the Army. Sometime later he made an improvement on the sight. His family said he was rewarded for his invention by being promoted from a buck private to major, at which time he retired from the Army. He was reported to have retired and moved to Hawaii.

Whether any part of the story about the invention is true is a matter of speculation.

However, true or not, what matters is that it is a great story about an event within the realm of possibility, a thing that could conceivably have happened. The point of the story is that dreams occur within everyone; we need only reach out our hands, grasp the idea in that dream, and follow through on it.

If you will use one percent of your capacity, you will become the greatest in your field and maybe in the world.

Bob Richards

Very, very few of us, if any, ever use anywhere near all of our potential. What we are capable of is awesome just to reflect upon. In his book *The Other 90%*, Robert Cooper says, "Studies now show that we use not one tenth but one ten-thousandth of our capacity." The Bible provides a succinct explanation of this in Mark 9:13: "All things are possible to them that believe." We can make ourselves believe anything by telling ourselves repeatedly, "I can, I will, I know there is a way, and I know I will find it."

You may say, but I'm not an Einstein, a Newton, or a Thomas Edison. Those men had no advantage over others. Each of us has just as much potential for greatness in the area or the realm of our aptitude as the individuals mentioned above had. Even Bill Gates, the computer genius, had no more potential for greatness than you have.

"How can I use more of my potential?" you may ask. There is one single key to achievement. This key will overcome any obstacle, open any door, solve any problem, and achieve any goal. It is the exact same key used by all achievers, great and small. There is simply no other way to accomplish anything.

This all-powerful key is your thinking. One uses his thinking and his imagination to impress his goals upon his subconscious mind, thereby programming himself. The human mind is so powerful it is completely incomprehensible. On January 3, 1999, *Us Weekly* had this to say:

> Even as you read these words, your brain is analyzing and processing information with an alacrity that makes the world's fastest computer seem like a baby's toy in comparison. The minimum number of possible thought patterns a psychologist once calculated, is the number 1, followed by 6 1/2 miles of typed zeroes.

Wow! What a marvel the human brain is! And you own one!

The beauty of the situation is, we have all this potential and we are allowed to tap into it through our ability to think. One of our greatest privileges is that we get to choose our every thought. When we choose positive thoughts, we program ourselves to get positive results. When we choose negative thoughts, we program ourselves to get negative results. Why not always choose positive thoughts and thereby always program ourselves to get positive results?

To know is nothing; to imagine is everything.

Anatole France

Nothing can be accomplished until it is seen in the mind, until it is imagined. Jules Verne, who conceived the idea of the airplane and the submarine a hundred years before they were invented, is credited with having said something to this effect: "Anything one mind can conceive, another mind can achieve."

There is a story of a sculptor that sculpted a lion from a huge stone. A little girl saw the sculptor at work. She said to the sculptor, "I didn't know there was a lion in that stone." The sculptor knew, however, because he could see it. In his imagination the lion was as well formed before he touched the stone with his tools as it was when he completed the job. If he had not seen it, he could not have sculpted it.

A sculptor, a woodcarver, a house builder, a seamstress, or any sort of creator has to have a model, a blueprint, or pattern in order to do the job. The model can be imaginary or it can be physical. An attempt to create anything without some plan to guide you or keep you in line would result in the creation of some kind of monstrosity. Everything that is invented or created first has to be an idea, a model in someone's mind.

Perhaps the most outstanding example of the power of the imagination in all of history was when President John F. Kennedy came up with the idea of putting a man on the moon. This idea first had to be seen in someone's mind. There had to be a pattern. There has to be something to guide people, some pattern or plan that they can see in their minds; otherwise they cannot make it happen.

Chapter 3:

Programming the Mind

The "self-image" is the key to human person-ality and human behavior. Change the self-image and you change the personality and the behavior.

Dr. Maxwell Maltz

The way we see ourselves is the most important aspect of our lives. How well or how poorly one does in school and how well or how poorly one does in life after school are not due to great intelligence or the lack of it. I began a career as a salesman, a type of work that was completely new to me. I knew absolutely nothing about being a salesman. I had never sold anything before in my life. I had dropped out of school after completing the sixth grade and was perhaps one of the shyest individuals around.

Despite all of those negatives, I was sure I would succeed. The mental image I held was one of complete success. By quoting to myself the third, fifth, seventh and last verses of Longfellow's poem "A Psalm of Life," the positive assertions in those verses helped me to do a magnificent job of programming myself for success.

> *Not enjoyment and not sorrow,*
> *Is our destin'd end or way;*
> *But to act, that each tomorrow*
> *Find us farther than today.*

> In the world's broad field of battle,
> In the bivouac of life,
> Be not like dumb, driven cattle!
> Be a hero in the strife!
>
> Lives of great men all remind us
> We can make our lives sublime,
> And, departing, leave behind us
> Footsteps on the sands of time.
>
> Let us then be up and doing,
> With a heart for any fate;
> Still achieving, still pursuing,
> Learn to labor and to wait.

When one becomes programmed, he simply changes his self-image. Also, when he is programmed to be more, do more and have more, he has perfect self-confidence. He has greatly enhanced his self-image. He knows without a shadow of a doubt that he will succeed. It is as if he has the evidence of success already before him.

In his book *Psychocybernetics*, Dr. Maltz also said,

> This self-image becomes a golden key
> to living a better life because of two

important discoveries:

All your actions, feelings, behavior—
even your abilities—are always consistent
with this self-image. In short you "will
act" like the sort of person you conceive
yourself to be. Not only this, but you literally cannot act otherwise, in spite of all
your conscious effort or will power. The
man who conceives himself to be a
"failure-type person" will find some way
to fail, in spite of all his good intentions or
will power, even if opportunity is literally
dumped in his lap....

The self-image can be changed;
numerous case histories have shown that
no one is ever too young or too old to
change his self-image and thereby start to
live a new life.

It is comforting to know we can change at any
age, that we are never too young or too old. At age
forty-four George Foreman changed his self-image
and became the heavyweight boxing champion of
the world. At age eighty-eight I changed my self-
image several times. At that advanced age I

changed my self-image and learned to use a computer, a change that enabled me to take a typing course and learn to type. That same year at age eighty-eight, I again changed my self-image and became the host of a radio program.

One of our most important heritages has to be our ability to change from what we are to whatever we would most like to be. This is done by the simple process of programming ourselves and thereby changing the mental image we hold of ourselves.

One would be almost bound to think that making such an important change would be difficult. But it is not difficult at all. Have a goal and program yourself to achieve it, by telling yourself over and over, "I can, I will; I know there is a way, and I know I will find it."

It is not likely to happen in a day or a week. You will need to give yourself this positive message many times a day until your subconscious accepts it. It may take thousands of repetitions. The day will come when you will see a great opportunity. This will change your self-image. When you change your self-image you change your attitude. To a great degree you could even say that you become a different person. If you are a failure type, this will transform you into a success type.

It is the mind that makes good or ill, that makes wretch or happy, rich or poor.

Edmund Spencer

This quote by Edmund Spencer is a profound statement of truth. The mental image we hold of ourselves gives us our attitude. Our attitude makes us what we are. The most successful among us become successful because they have a positive attitude. The most miserable failure among us fails because of a negative attitude.

One of our most important privileges is that we have the ability to change our attitude. In fact, it is not only a privilege, it is a must. We, by nature, must develop, select, choose, create or determine our attitude. How we react to the things that happen to us is much more important than the thing that happened. We always have a choice. We always react the way we decide to. And the way we decide is determined by our attitude.

When he was ten or eleven years old, a grandson of mine, Tom, was showing a headstrong horse in what would be classed as a low-grade horse show. The horse made a bobble and my grandson fell off. This was right out in the middle ring. He had a choice to make. Most of the people watching would surely have thought he would leave the ring embarrassed. He did not do that. He climbed right back on the horse and finished the show. The attitude that led him to get back on the horse and finish the show has carried him far. He now travels all over America as an auctioneer and sells thoroughbred and saddlebred horses. He also travels far and wide to judge horse shows.

There's more. He is also in the real estate business in Kentucky. He has sold some of the best farms in that state at auction. When Tom fell off the horse he made the kind of choice anyone in a similar situation could have made. That type of attitude helped to make him the happy, successful person he is today.

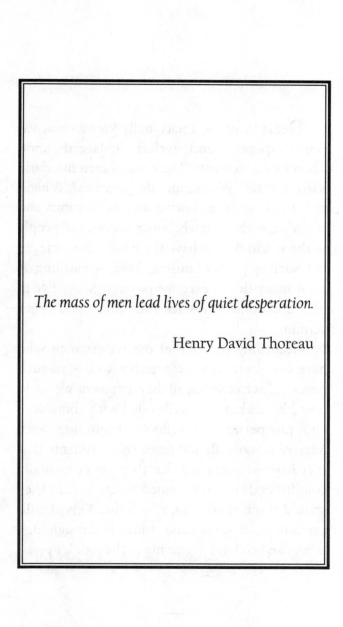

The mass of men lead lives of quiet desperation.

Henry David Thoreau

Denis Waitley, a nationally known motivational speaker and writer, enlarged upon Thoreau's statement: "The mass of men live dark, narrow little lives of quiet desperation." What a pity. In a world overflowing with opportunity and abundance, the overwhelming majority of people in the world do not have the basic necessities of life, such as proper housing, food, or clothing. A great many live in extreme poverty. Many live in filth and some live with rats, mice, and other vermin.

According to some of the wisest men who have ever lived, no one ever has to live in such poverty. Each of us has all the equipment we could possibly need to have a life filled with abundance and prosperity. All schools, beginning with nursery schools, should teach their students that they have no limits and that they can be mentally conditioned or programmed to excel, and they should teach them how it is done. This should begin in grade school and continue through high school and college. Beginning in the toddler years, it should be taught in the home throughout childhood and all the way into adulthood.

Arthur Brisbane, a syndicated columnist whose writings reached 30,000,000 readers back in the 1920s, said, "Nothing has been said until it has been said a thousand times." That being true, children should be told on a regular basis that they have what it takes to excel. And that they *can* excel. This would promote high self-esteem. Having great belief in themselves, they would likely excel in some field.

Instead, most hear the exact opposite throughout their childhood: "You can't, you are too little, you're not old enough, you'll get hurt, you'll fall and break a leg, or you'll catch your death of cold." Many are called stupid or dumb— or worse. Since children do not know how to thwart those negative statements, they are usually affected by them for their entire lives.

The end result is a person with a poor self-image and a poor attitude and with little belief in himself and his abilities. This person, therefore, is programmed for failure and joins the masses that "live dark, narrow little lives of quiet desperation."

By far the most important thing about you is the unlimited mental resources you were born with and have within you right now. You are perfectly equipped to become whatever you most want to be, or to do, or to have what you most want to have. Your mind is as fertile, as creative, and as capable as any mind that ever existed in mortal man. You are a distinctly unique person who has many special talents and an ability which you can use to excel in some endeavor, if that is what you wish to do. Many people with no more talent or ability than you have, have gained world renown for their inventions, ideas, and inspirations.

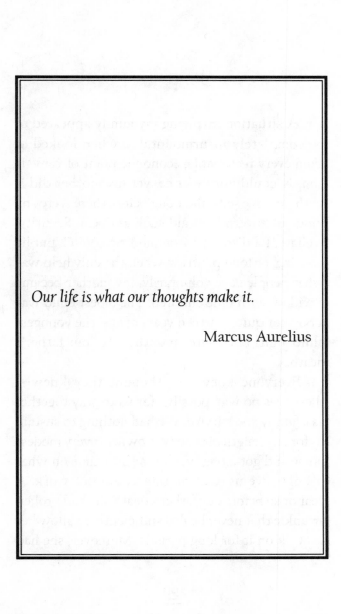

Our life is what our thoughts make it.

Marcus Aurelius

A situation involving my family appeared to be completely insurmountable when looked at from every reasonable, economic point of view. It simply could not be done, yet my mother did it with positive self-talk. Long before there were any kinds of government aid such as Social Security, welfare, food stamps, commodities, WIC, public housing, or food pantries, when the only help was what people gave voluntarily, my mother became a widow with nine children. The oldest child was a boy not quite thirteen years of age, the youngest child a girl born three months after our father's death.

Everyone knew—or thought they knew—there was no way possible for us to stay together as a family and survive. We had nothing to sustain us for any length of time. We owned a very modest home and got along well for a short time on what people gave us. Our mother could not work. A year or so before our father's death she had broken an ankle that never healed sufficiently to allow her to walk on it for long periods. Moreover, she had no training that would enable her to get a job to earn money.

As soon as our father was buried, both of our grandmothers, an aunt, a great aunt and an uncle came to our home for a family conference to decide what to do with us children, who would take which child to raise. When they had us divided, my mother said, "I'm not going to do that yet," which meant two things. She had desire, perhaps as compelling as desire can possibly be, to keep her family together. She also had a faint glimmer of hope.

She began to claim, "God is a father to the orphans and a husband to the widows." She told us that many, many times a day, day in and day out. Where the statement came from is anyone's guess. It is not in the Bible, but it is implied there. However, in the beginning, she only believed this intellectually. She did not believe strongly enough emotionally to act on it. Had she believed it strongly there would have been no need for the family conference. She was not only telling us children; she was claiming it for herself. She was programming herself or developing faith, which is actually the same thing. This went on for three, possibly four weeks.

One morning everything was different. She was ecstatic. She had developed the emotional belief, or one could say an unshakable faith, that she could keep her family together. A door had opened that she had not known was there. She could see possibilities and potential that she had not been able to see before.

We got along surprisingly well. All things seemed to work together for our communal good. We always had plenty of food and clothing, along with the other necessities of life. We continued to live as well as we had been living on the wages our father had earned as a skilled worker.

My mother had tapped an inexhaustible source that is always available to everyone. She had complete confidence that all things would continue to be all right because she had the faith and strong emotional conviction to believe without doubt or question. She had done a masterful job of programming herself.

There are two ways to believe: intellectually and emotionally. I once heard an imaginary story about a tightrope walker illustrating the difference between the two ways of believing. According to the story, he had walked ropes all around the country and was well known because of his ability to do so. He decided to put on a spectacular show and push a wheelbarrow across Niagara Falls on a wire. He had a wire stretched across the falls. A mass of people gathered to see it. He asked for a showing of hands of everyone who thought he could do it. Because of his record, most held their hands high. But when he asked for a volunteer to ride in the wheelbarrow, no one would. They were all too fearful since they believed it only intellectually.

To believe intellectually does not mean much. However, when one believes emotionally, he has no fear and is programmed to attempt feats that would appear to be impossible. Then one has perfect confidence. Figuratively speaking, he will get into the wheelbarrow.

My mother, who had no visible means of support, did what would be equal to getting into the wheelbarrow. We had a milk cow and a heifer, which soon became a cow. In a few months, she somehow acquired another cow. We had a dependable income from this mini-dairy. Since there was no law to prevent it, our cows were free to roam the countryside. My older brother and I got jobs as custodians of the school we were attending, earning twenty dollars a month. The combined income from all our efforts enabled us to live quite well.

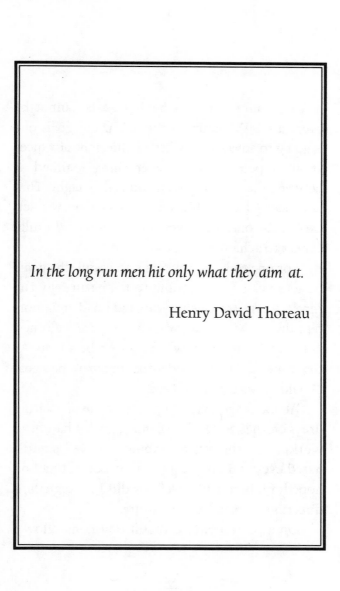

In the long run men hit only what they aim at.

Henry David Thoreau

The importance of having goals cannot be overstated. Without specific, clear-cut goals one is going to advance very little in life, if he advances at all. I personally hit everything I aimed at between the ages of fifteen and eighty-eight. That is to say I have achieved every goal I ever set, except the ones I am working on now and I fully expect to achieve those, too.

For one to be happy and successful, the goals he sets must be according to his nature. By the time I was ten or twelve years old I had an important dream. My dream was to wear dress clothes, not overalls, to work when I got to be a man. At that time I did not consider that dream to be a goal I could, in actuality, achieve.

At about age twenty-one my dream of wearing dress clothes to work became a goal. I had been working on the railroad about two years and I hated every minute of it. At that point, I had no hope for a better life. Neither did I have goals, a direction, or plans for the future.

On a particularly difficult day Longfellow's

poem "A Psalm of Life" came to my mind. The four stanzas I mentioned earlier changed my life. They sounded so good I continued to quote them for many months. Quoting the positive statements in the verses finally caused me to develop hope. Once I had hope, the desire to wear dress clothes became a goal.

At the same time, I became aware of two other compatible goals. I did not set those goals. They were already there, within me; I just discovered them. The first was to leave the railroad for good. The second was to sleep in my own bed every night. I did not want to travel.

I did not know of anything I could do or any move I could make to achieve my goals. The verses of the poem sounded so good I continued to quote them for several more months. I then had a wonderful, life-changing experience. I had a new attitude, a new self-image, and a new outlook on life. The verses thoroughly programmed me for success.

Like all of the other goals I have set, I got a lot more than I expected. I left the railroad for good, got work where I wore dress clothes, did not have to travel, and increased my income sixfold. Had I not aimed at those goals I would not have hit them.

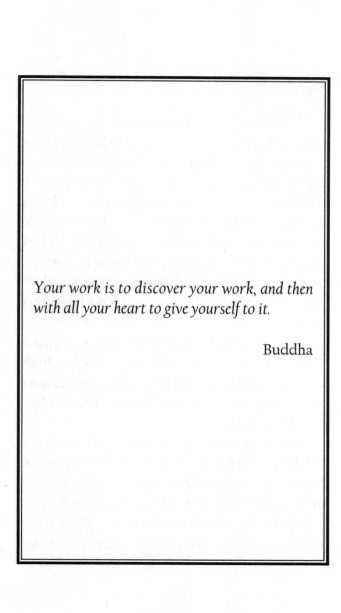

Your work is to discover your work, and then with all your heart to give yourself to it.

Buddha

Thinkers and philosophers of the past have said each of us has our special talent and that these talents were given to us to use. Students of human behavior now say that a very small percentage of us ever find our true place in life or find the work we were born to do. Those who do not find their work are facing a lifetime of toil. Those that find their work love doing it. They get great psychological fulfillment by doing it. As Mark Twain said, "If you like to do it, it ain't work."

Everyone should begin searching for his place in life at an early age and never let up until he finds it. Once he finds it he will be able to do more, serve his fellow man better, and have a richer, fuller, more rewarding life.

To find your true place in life—the work you will love—decide what is the most important change you would like to see take place in your life as of right now or in the near future. Whatever it is, write it down. Read it often. Tell yourself repeatedly, "I can, I will, I know there is a way for me to bring this change about, and I know I will find it." Practice this technique. Stick with it. It will work.

You might ask, "How will I know when I have found it?" That is easy. When you find work that you love to do, you have arrived at the right place.

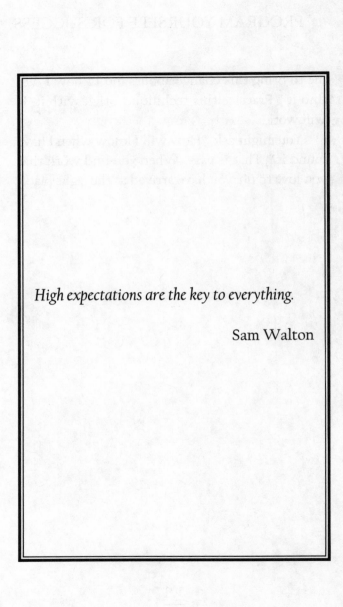

High expectations are the key to everything.

Sam Walton

Being resolute in your expectations is the key to succeeding at the goals you have set for your self. History, in fact, teaches the truth of this statement. It is no wonder Sam Walton became the owner of more stores than anyone else in the world. He undoubtedly reached a place in life where he expected to own numerous stores. He undoubtedly made up his mind that he would do so no matter what. This determination did not permit him to look either to the right or to the left. It demanded that he keep his eye firmly on his goal.

In 1933, the worst year of the Great Depression of the 1930s, when 25.2 percent of the American work force was unemployed, I left a secure job on a railroad and took a job with the Fuller Brush Company as a door-to-door sales-man. There was no salary or guaranteed income. The pay was straight commission. Despite the fact that I was extremely shy and had never sold anything before, I knew without the slightest doubt that I would succeed. I not only succeeded,

I did far better than I had hoped. I immediately increased my income 600 percent.

The Longfellow poem, along with several other occurences, thoroughly conditioned my mind—or programmed me to succeed. The Fuller Brush salesman who had called on us for years always dressed well, drove a good car, and lived in one of the best homes in the area. I thought being with that company offered great opportunity. I had a strong belief in the company, in the products they were manufacturing and in their method of doing business. With such a belief my success was almost guaranteed. Once the idea took hold I was sure I would do well.

When I left the store and started selling automobiles, I had programmed myself so thoroughly that I knew I would succeed. The same was true when I began my real estate career. Again I knew I would be successful. When our first son was born the doctor said, "It's a boy." When I heard those words I had a thought that had never before entered my mind: that this boy would graduate from college. I was working at a salary of only $85.00 a month. Five and a half years later we were blessed with another son. I went through the exact same process. The doctor said, "It's a boy." I knew those boys would graduate from college as much as I knew they were human beings. I was not at all surprised when each of them enrolled in college, did very well and graduated. They did exactly as I had expected them to do.

Churchill expected to win the war against Germany, and he certainly did. General Douglas MacArthur, in the Philippines, said, "I shall return." He expected to return and he did exactly that. The great John Paul Jones said, "I have not yet begun to fight." He expected to win and, unsurprisingly, he won. Success is never a surprise to anyone who has programmed himself to succeed.

Every act of man springs from the hidden seeds of thought and could not appear without them. The outer world of circumstance shapes itself to the inner world of thought. All that a man achieves and all that he fails to achieve is the direct result of his own thoughts.

James Allen

People have had full measures of success by using their imagination, by visualizing, by pretending in their minds that they were already successfully doing the thing they really wanted to do and being the kind of persons they really wanted to be. Jack Nicklaus, one of the greatest golfers of all time, thoroughly programmed himself by using his imagination. When he was only about ten years of age, he began to see himself as a great golfer. He pictured himself playing with the greatest golfers and winning. In his imagination he heard radio announcers describing him as a great champion. This went on for a period of months, maybe years.

Eventually, the pictures he had held in his mind became a reality, as they always do. He won the state amateur tournament five times, as well as the national amateur title of the U.S. Golf Association and the U.S. Open Golf tournament the year he turned professional. He was the first to win $100,000 in one year, the first to amass winnings of $1,000,000, and the first to win the

Masters tournament four times. He won the professional association championship five times and the British Open Tournament three times. In 1962 and 1964 he was named golfer of the year. He was also named golfer of the decade. He became the man he had programmed himself to become.

Nicklaus' outer world of circumstance certainly shaped itself to his inner world of thought. Your outer world of circumstance always shapes itself to your inner world of thought. It is up to you to take advantage of that fact.

Whatever is maintained as an image in the mind will make its way into the outer world and manifest itself as a physical fact.

Robert Collier

It is possible for you to use the power of the imagination to maintain your abilities and focus your goals even in the worst of circumstances. This fact is illustrated by Senator John McCain of Arizona, who for five and a half years was a prisoner of war in Vietnam. He was an avid golfer capable of playing par golf. In prison for all those years with nothing to do, he imagined himself playing the game. It has been reported that he mentally played a round every day.

He surely would have played a good game, almost always putting the ball near where he wanted it to go. Almost every drive would have been a good one; every pitch and every chip would have also been good, and every putt would have gone into or near the cup. All golfers, even the professionals, must play regularly in order to maintain their expertise, their sharpness. Shortly after his release from prison, McCain played a round of golf. Thanks to his years of mental imaging, he had not lost his ability and was still able to play at par.

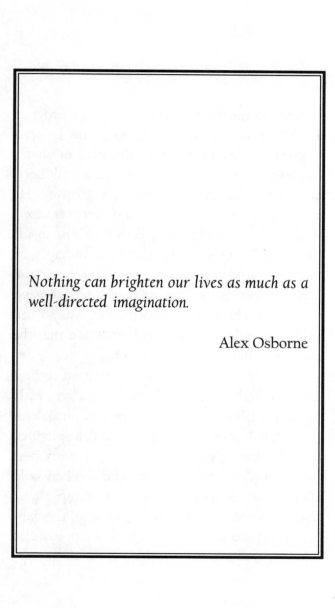

Nothing can brighten our lives as much as a well-directed imagination.

Alex Osborne

According to an interview on the TV program *20/20*, Bob "Butter Bean" Love, one of the greatest basketball players that ever dribbled or shot a basketball, experienced a very bleak childhood and had little hope for a promising future. He grew up in the home of his grandmother along with twelve other kids in a house with no inside plumbing. Besides all the other disadvantages, he had a severe speech impediment, stammering so badly it was almost impossible for him to get a word out. This speech impediment was so bad that he hated to go to school, knowing that the other boys would make fun of him.

He knew, however, that he wanted to be a great basketball player. He began at a very early age to use his imagination to program himself for greatness. At night as he lay in his bed, he pictured himself playing with and beating the very best professional players. In his imagination he would slam-dunk on them, make great jump shots, always outplay them. He could hear the fans screaming and see the clock run down to that last second.

He really got the message over to his subconscious mind. He fully programmed himself. When that was accomplished, this image was bound to become a reality in his life, and it did.

Love got a scholarship to Southern University, where he was an All-American three years in a row. He then played for the Chicago Bulls and was their top scorer for seven years and an all-pro for three years. Despite his great performances, most fans knew little about him because he got few write-ups on the sports pages and in sports magazines. Sports writers did not interview him due to the problems with his speech. He was a great star on the floor, but when the game was over, his day was done.

Since he did not earn big money endorsing products as other players did, he was broke soon after retiring from the game and found it necessary to find another source of income. Because of his inability to communicate well, he was unable to get a high-paying job. This forced him to accept a job as a busboy in a hotel where he earned very low pay, a far cry from his glory days on the basketball court. In spite of the embarrassment it caused him and the meager salary, he tried to be the best busboy he could be.

Still his speech problem plagued him night and day. Once, attempting to make a speech, he stood for several agonizing minutes and not a word would come out. He was hurt and embarrassed. That night as he lay in his bed, he began to use his imagination again, forming mental pictures of himself as a great speaker. Sometimes he would see himself as Martin Luther King, Jr., other times as President John F. Kennedy. In his imagination, his voice was clear and smooth.

Those dreams were so real that he could see the people looking at him, giving him their full attention. Night after night, it was as if he were watching movies of himself as a great speaker. Those mental pictures fully programmed him to be a successful speaker. Again, a great infallible law of nature decreed that it had to become a reality. He had to be able to speak.

As a result of his dedication and loyalty, he attracted the attention of his employer, who, upon learning of his disability, wanted to help him and agreed to pay the cost of speech therapy. Fortunately, he received the services of a top-quality therapist. He worked hard and was soon speaking fluently.

When he developed the ability to talk, his old team, the Bulls, rehired him as their community relations specialist. That meant his occupation was speaking. He spoke all around the country to schools, clubs and other groups, encouraging others to dream big dreams.

A well-directed imagination will brighten your life, as it did the life of Bob "Butter Bean" Love.

There are no bounds to the possibility of man.

Ralph Waldo Emerson

According to a story in Pete Axthelm's book *The Kid* , Steve Cauthin, the most celebrated jockey in all racing history, began winning races as soon as he was old enough to ride. He rode his first winner seventeen days after his sixteenth birthday. The year he was seventeen he won more races and more money than had ever been won in one year by any other jockey. He was the youngest rider ever to win $6,000,000 in one year. That same year he was the youngest jockey ever to win the most important prize in racing, the Triple Crown.

There were stories about him on sports pages and in sports magazines all over America and abroad. The Associated Press, *Sporting News*, and *Sports Illustrated* named him Sportsman of the Year. In fact, almost every sports organization that gave an annual prize presented it to Cauthin. All of this happened to the greatest of all jockeys before his eighteenth birthday.

Continuing to win, he won the English, French, and Irish derbies and became the first

American to win all the major international thoroughbred races. The likes of him had never been seen before.

How did he accomplish all of this? Steve Cauthin had done a magnificent job of programming himself. At about age twelve he told his father he wanted to be a jockey and began to use his imagination, pretending that he was the greatest jockey that had ever lived.

His family had a few acres of land on which sat a small barn with a hayloft. Steve would go to the hayloft, straddle a bale of hay, and pretend it was a horse winning the most important races. He nailed leather lines to the wall pretending that they were bridle reins, and he spent hundreds of hours winning imaginary races with his imaginary steeds.

When he was busy with schoolwork and other things, he would go to the barn in the middle of the night and ride for hours. He practiced using the reins to control his horse. He actually used a regular riding whip, beating up many bales of hay, learning just how to hold it, how to change hands with it, how to hit the horse in the same place in the flank with every lick. His mental pictures of success made him the greatest jockey ever.

Cauthin proved to himself that there were no bounds to his possibilities. You too can prove to yourself that there are no bounds to your possibilities.

PROGRAM YOURSELF FOR SUCCESS

The power to move the world is in your subconscious mind. Whatever you impress on your subconscious, the latter will move heaven and earth to bring it to pass.

William James

What happened to my son, Ben Jr., sounds like a miracle. He was in the last year of high school, and in all his prior schooling, he had never made an A, except in non-academics such as music and gymnastics, and he had made only two B's. He then began listening to motivational records. Tapes had not yet come into wide use. He did not listen just once, twice or a hundred times. He listened to the records hundreds and hundreds of times. He rigged a player so it would play the same record over and over. He listened to the records all night, every night, for three or four months. He played them until they were completely worn out and until not a word on them could be understood.

They poured positive thoughts into his mind as he was going to sleep, as he was waking up and all night long, every night. The records told him many, many times what a great, powerful and creative mind he had, that nothing was beyond him, and that the world was overflowing with abundance and opportunities. Listening to all those positive assertions transformed Ben Jr. from someone who saw himself as weak and lacking in competence, skill, and ability into someone who saw himself as extremely capable.

Because thoughts we allow into our minds have such transforming effects on our behavior and our lives, listening to those records so changed him that he was now a different person. He developed great belief in himself and his abilities. He had two more grading periods in high school and made straight A's.

Listening to those records affected every area of his life. In college, he was president, vice president, and social chairman of his fraternity and president of the Inter-Fraternity Council. He was a member of Omicron Delta Kappa, the national men's leadership fraternity, and a member of The Robe, a men's leadership fraternity. Only about twenty students at his school received that honor in each of these fraternities.

Ben Jr. was a student governor, a dean's list student, president of the senior class, and was listed in *Who's Who in American Colleges and Universities*. Only thirty other students at the school received that honor. He graduated *cum laude* from The Ohio State University Law School. According to an article in *The Columbus Monthly*, he is now one of two lawyers in the field of real estate in the city of Columbus that are recommended by other lawyers.

Ben Jr. had no advantage over you or anyone else. You have as much ability to change your self-image, your attitude, and your circumstances as he had.

Chapter 4:

Setting and Following Your Goals

The person who makes a success in life is the one who sees his goal steadily and aims for it unswervingly. That is dedication.

Cecil B. De Mille

How could one strive for something if he did not see what he was striving for? He must see his goal steadily and strive for it tenaciously. A person not having a precise goal would be like a ship putting out to sea without sailing orders or a destination. If one does not know where he is going, he can never reach his destination because he will never know when or whether he has arrived.

A boy grew up on a small hillside farm and was the next to oldest of eleven children of a very poor family. His father was not really able to work, making it necessary, despite the number of children, for his mother to work outside of their home doing domestic work. When he was in grade school he began talking about going to college. He knew he wanted to be a teacher. There didn't appear to be a chance in a million that he would ever be able to go to high school, let alone get into college. Going to college appeared to be a complete impossibility.

I was closely associated with this individual

when he was in the eighth grade. I did my best to convince him that he was building himself up for a big letdown. And those are the exact words I used. My talk was totally ineffective.

He and I remained close friends, and as it turned out, he proved me wrong. He became an inspiration to me. He was as goal-oriented and as tenacious as one could be. He managed to go to high school and did his very best as a student. He always made good grades. Not the best, but very good. He was never a problem for any of his teachers. He was considered the most dedicated student in that school.

For these and other outstanding qualities a woman's club in the area gave him a $25.00 scholarship, which was the cost of one semester in a nearby college. When the time came he enrolled in the college despite several formidable barriers that seemed to prohibit him from attending.

The school was seven miles from his home, and the only way he had to get there was to walk. There was a river to cross on a ferry at a cost of five cents each way. He did not have the ten cents. That would have stopped most people. Not him.

Every day he asked someone with horses and a wagon or someone in a car to let him ride over with them. Since the number of people in the vehicle didn't affect the charge, most people would give him a ride.

He had no books. He depended on good notes and library books. That is until the woman's club that had given him the scholarship learned about the situation and loaned him money to buy books. He braved the freezing cold, the snowy and rainy weather, and completed that first semester. Paying for the next semester was an enormous task. It became a family project. They managed to gather the money only because several family members contributed what they could.

He made it through the first two semesters with flying colors. The next fall he received a huge reward and got a chance to sample the kind of life he had always wanted and for which he had paid so dearly. He got a job teaching in a one-room country school.

That was just the beginning of a very successful and happy life. He continued teaching and going to school. He taught during the day and went to school in the evenings and during the summers. But he no longer had to walk. He now drove to that one-room school and to his classes.

He eventually earned a master's degree and more. In the school system where he taught, being a superintendent required certain academic qualifications beyond a master's degree. Always looking to the future, he wanted to be ready if the opportunity to be a county superintendent of schools ever came his way, so he took the required courses. He became the principal of a grade school, later on the principal of a high school, and finally superintendent of schools in the county in which he had taught.

This person certainly saw his goal steadily and aimed for it unswervingly.

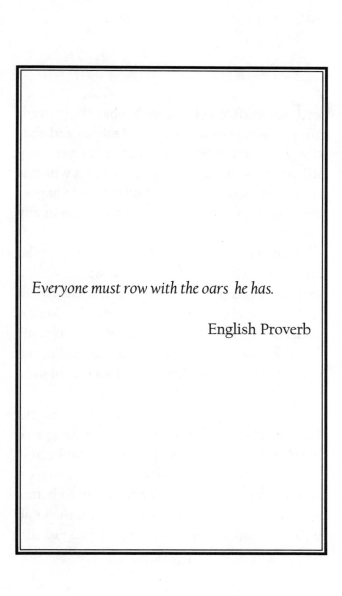

Everyone must row with the oars he has.

English Proverb

Each of us was born with what the proverb refers to as oars—certain natural talents and abilities. Some were born to function in narrowly defined areas and can do well in the area which is natural for them, but would find it next to impossible to find much success or satisfaction in any other area.

An individual we will call Matt was a boy who did not do well in school. When he was in school, no student was promoted to a higher grade unless he was capable of doing the work. Matt's academic ability was limited. When he quit school he was almost a man and was still in the fourth grade. *But he had oars, special oars,* in another area. He was very skilled in mechanics.

By the time he left school he owned an old claptrap of a car that was always in danger of dying on the road, yet Matt was able to keep it running. His only employment was working on automobiles. As he got older he acquired better cars. When coal was first trucked from the mine to the railroad, where it was loaded into railroad cars, the trucks that were used were not very big. Matt somehow managed to become the owner of a truck that was old and in poor condition. But, again, because of his mechanic ability, he was able to keep it on the road.

He rowed with the oars he had. He continued to row. In a few years he owned six or eight of those huge eighteen-wheelers, one of which could haul as much as fifty tons of coal. The cost of such a truck was well over $100,000. Remaining loyal to his natural talents and abilities served him and his family very well. He put himself in a position to be happy, feel secure and enjoy life, and thus helped his wife and children do the same.

If you make good use of your natural talents and abilities, you can become a success just like Matt.

Few things are impossible, and we lack the application to make them a success rather than the will.

La Rochefoucauld

There was a successful businessman who, even as a boy, had always applied himself, even in sports. In high school football he played hard. As a result he was made captain of his team. He also made very good grades. Upon graduating high school he was given a scholarship to play football in college.

His father owned a successful small business and also owned one of the best homes in the neighborhood. Because of a serious tragedy in the family, the father sold the business and the home and spent all the money to resolve the problem, but to no avail. The family was forced to move to a less-impressive home. The home they moved to was so inferior to the home in which they had lived that the football player was ashamed for his teammates to know where he lived.

He decided then that he would own a brick house and have it paid for before he would get married. This was a vow that demonstrated his character. He did not plan to put marriage off for years, but planned to take a wife while he was still a very young man.

Because of the economic conditions of the country, his goal appeared to be an impossible dream. That was in the 1930s and right in the middle of the worst depression this country had ever experienced. But here was a young man ready to apply himself and make his dream a reality.

He did not like the circumstances he found at school and soon returned home. Because of his remarkably optimistic attitude, returning home was not a mistake. Before he left college he discovered within himself a powerful idea, an idea that served him extremely well for years and finally led him into a career that placed him among the most successful in his chosen field, automobile mechanics.

He decided that he would work on automobiles as a body man. That is, he would repair the bodies of cars that had been wrecked. His idea was that he would go to a body shop with a good reputation and offer to work for free until he became so valuable to them that they would hire him. The body shop not only gave him a job, they started him at a salary of $15.00 a week, which was fairly good pay at that time for a person just starting out. In a few years he was regarded as one of the best body men in the area.

Very soon after he began repairing car bodies, he got a part-time job as an agent with an insurance company which, to some degree, specialized in automobile insurance, but which also sold life and fire insurance. Many evenings after the shop where he worked closed for the day, he was out selling automobile insurance. As it turned out, he was very successful at selling insurance.

After a few years working for others he opened a body shop of his own, which became very prosperous. He also continued his insurance business on the side, and that company continued to prosper as well.

He was considered to be a top-quality body man and had one of the most successful businesses of that type in the area for a number of years. Meanwhile, his insurance business continued to grow. The time came for him to leave the shop and go into the insurance business full-time, where he enjoyed phenomenal success. He did so well that his company, which normally placed three or more agents in a county, would not place any agent other than him in his county. In almost every case, when he sold a policy he made a friend who immediately began recommending him.

Although his goal of owning and paying off a brick home before getting married appeared to be almost impossible, he made it happen. When he reached age twenty-three he married his high school sweetheart. They started a household in their very own, new, attractive brick home, which they owned free and clear.

He not only achieved his original goal by applying himself; he achieved other goals that were within the realm of his aptitudes. By applying himself and investing wisely, he became one of the individuals in the top two or three percent bracket of the most successful citizens in America.

This young man was willing to start at the bottom and do the best he could. He took advantages of opportunities as they presented themselves. There is nothing keeping you from doing the same and eventually ending up at the top.

Chiefly the mold of a man's fortune is in his own hands.

Francis Bacon

A young man in Syria had a dream—to come to America and to go into business as his uncle had done. What he had was more than a dream. It was an obsession. As soon as he was able to come up with sufficient fare to make the trip, he set out on what would appear to be an impossible task. When he landed in America he could speak no English, had never even as much as heard the language spoken. His success depended on his ability to use the language to communicate.

His uncle owned a wholesale business in the Midwest. He handled all sorts of products related to the home, including clothing for the entire family and all other types of domestic dry goods and textiles. When the young man from Syria arrived at his destination in America, he had only one nickel. His uncle had agreed to let him have merchandise for which he could pay as it was sold. His idea was to sell the merchandise house to house, door to door, which was a common practice then, because most families had no transportation to get to the stores to buy what they needed. Despite the fact that the young man from Syria could not speak any English, he took an assortment of merchandise, as much as he could carry, and began his new business.

Men that used that method of selling were called pack peddlers, because the enormous amount of merchandise they carried looked as if it were impossible for one man to handle. They carried two or three huge leather box-like containers with leather straps around them and around the shoulders of the peddlers. When their wares were displayed in the home, it was almost like being in a department store. This was an advantageous situation for both the salesman and the homemaker looking to buy goods.

He continued his peddling until enough families began getting automobiles and could drive to a store. He then opened a department store in town, which did well. He did not stop with one store. He continued adding stores, and long before reaching retirement age, he owned nine. Although it appeared to be impossible, the young man from Syria followed and acted on his dream and saw it become a reality.

Chapter 5:

Risk Is a Myth

The word "impossible" belongs only in the dictionary of fools.

Napoleon

A man we'll call Sam gave a talk at a luncheon. He told a moving story about something that he had thought he would dearly love to do but could see no possible way of doing. He worked for minimum wage as a clean-up man at a fast-food restaurant. According to his story, he came from far back in the rural part of the country and was so unattractive the manager would not let him work in the front part of the business. He had to remain in the back—with one exception. They would let him go out to the front of the building to clean the windows.

He worked there and observed how the business was managed. He imagined himself doing a better job of managing the store than the current manager was doing.

He eventually developed what would be called a passionate desire to own such a place, the cost of which would amount to hundreds of thousands of dollars. The thought of ever having that much money seemed completely out of the question for him, totally impossible. He continued to clean and to dream. He thought about it almost constantly. As he lay in bed at night he would visualize himself owning and managing one of the restaurants.

As time went on, things changed. He got to be a manager, and became a very successful manager at that. When he took over as manager, business picked up. He was later moved into a job with much greater responsibility: he was given the task of going out and finding locations for new restaurants.

He apparently was successful at that also. He was so successful, in fact, that another large chain of restaurants hired him away from his original company. In addition to seeking out locations for new restaurants, his new company sent him to temporarily manage restaurants where the profits were down. He must have had special skill in that area, for he always succeeded in his efforts.

Three partners owned one of the restaurants that got into trouble. He was sent to see if he could rescue the business. He was successful and in a short time the business was doing well. Later, however, the restaurant was doing poorly again.

He was sent to that same restaurant a second time. The men that owned it undoubtedly were very poor managers, so they called for him a third time. The third time he went back, one of the partners had sold his interest to the other two. He got the business doing well again. He was offered that third share of the business to come and manage the restaurant permanently. He accepted the offer, and the business flourished.

In a very short time he bought out the share of another partner. He then owned two-thirds of the business. The third partner offered to sell his share, and he took advantage of that offer. He now owned the business. He didn't stop, however, at owning just one restaurant. Within a few years he owned eight. They all did exceedingly well.

As it turned out, he did not need to raise hundreds of thousands of dollars in order to buy a restaurant. He didn't need to raise any money. But he got what he wanted and more. All he needed to do was to believe in his dream and apply himself to achieve it. He is now living that dream.

The moral of the story: never accept the concept that the thing you most want is impossible to get. It is not.

Man is nothing else but what he makes of himself.

Jean-Paul Sartre

A young man was married and the father of two young children. He could not find it within himself to settle for the average. He wanted a better life for his wife, his children, and himself. He decided to make something of himself. This was in the early part of the Great Depression of the 1930s. There did not appear to be very much opportunity for him to improve himself or his circumstances.

However, I have found this to be a rule of life: the condition of the national economy has little or nothing to do with whether there is opportunity for one to improve oneself financially.

Instead of sitting idly by, this young man did something. He took a correspondence course in accounting. He applied himself, studied diligently, and mastered the course, earning top grades.

When the course was finished he started a small business in order to gain experience as an accountant. He had a brother who had done some work as a plumber and who agreed to work for him. So the logical business in which to start was plumbing.

His intention from the very beginning was to do top-quality work and to treat every customer with the greatest respect. In the beginning, to guarantee their work the brothers took only simple, easy-to-do jobs.

From the start the plumbing business prospered. His new business soon grew to the point that one man could not do all the work. When that happened he quit his job as a meat cutter and started doing some of the simple plumbing jobs himself along with the bookkeeping. He was naturally skilled in mechanics. This helped him to learn the trade quickly. In a very short time he and his brother were first-class plumbers.

They did such high-quality work that they soon had most of the quality plumbing work in the area. Due to the increased business, the brothers needed a building with ample storage room in which they could also display their merchandise. He bought an attractive, well-situated brick building with a big glass front. He had the name of his company prominently displayed on the front of the building.

He had long since quit doing any of the plumbing or accounting himself. He was by this time a full-time manager of his plumbing company. He had hired a C.P.A to do his accounting and six or seven plumbers who worked for him by the hour.

He found it more profitable to cater to the community's plumbing needs than to take contracts to plumb huge new buildings. Therefore he served the community and served it well. With business continuing to do well, he purchased seven or eight half-ton pickup trucks that equipped him to serve the community even better.

He had made himself into a very successful businessman. By being unwilling to settle for the status quo, he was able to provide everything and more that his family needed. They owned a very adequate home, drove good automobiles, and sent their children to high-quality schools. It is amazing what you can make of yourself when you try. There is always opportunity.

I would sooner fail than not be among the greatest.

John Keats

Desiring to be among the greatest is an admirable trait. It is a desire that could take you far and be very rewarding. I had an older brother who, as we grew up, was so slow and particular about the way he did things that I was concerned he would never be able to earn his living. He was what is often referred to as a perfectionist. Everything he did had to be just right.

As a teenager he went to work in a railroad machine shop. He saw what the machinist did and knew that was what he wanted do for a living. Everything a machinist does has to be absolutely perfect. That greatly appealed to him. He just knew he had to become a machinist. He also knew he wanted to be among the greatest in his field. That was his true place in life.

He applied to the company he worked for to become a machinist apprentice. He was given that opportunity almost immediately. An apprenticeship of that sort normally required four years to complete. It took him six years to complete the apprenticeship because he did not get full-time work since this occurred during the Depression of the 1930s.

He did not earn very much money during those years, but received enormous pay in other ways. He simply delighted in working on things that could not vary more than one ten-thousandth of an inch. Working in such close tolerance gave him a kind of psychological fulfillment. He seemed to get a huge thrill by just talking about it.

When he had just a week to go to complete the apprenticeship and acquire a job as a machinist with the company for whom he was working, he quit his job. I thought he must have been out of his mind and told him so. He said, "No, I spent all that time, but I'm still not a machinist. The shop where I served my apprenticeship did not have all the machines I need to know about."

He was driven to be among the very best, and to do that, especially as a perfectionist, he felt he had to know how to work on every piece of equipment in his field. He went to the largest machine shop in the state and worked for two more years. Following those two years, he went to the second-largest machine shop in the state and worked another two years.

He came to visit me after completing the last two years. He said, "I'm a machinist. I can do anything any machinist can do, and I am going to wherever machinists receive the highest pay." He ended up working for Lockheed, the huge airplane factory in Marietta, Georgia, where he was paid very high wages.

He received other great benefits. Within a short time he was promoted to a toolmaker. A short time later he was promoted to a tool designer. Although he only had an eighth grade education, in about five years he was promoted to mechanical engineer, a profession he followed for the remainder of his working years.

Chapter 6:

*Like Yourself
and Treat Others Well*

Nothing is at last sacred but the integrity of your own mind. Absolve yourself, and you shall have the suffrage of the world.

Emerson

There is nothing more important to someone who is starting out in life and is desirous of becoming a highly successful, honorable, well-to-do and well-respected member of society than maintaining impeccable integrity. One should absolve oneself from all feelings of guilt. In other words, always do what you know to be right, and you shall have the vote of the world. You will build a reputation, and the whole world will be for you. The people you need to support you in your venture will beat a path to your door.

One of the most important things in life is to think well of one's self. To achieve and maintain that feeling, one must be totally and completely honest in all his dealings. Dealing with the public for more than fifty years, I found most people to be totally honest and pleasant to deal with. When I was just a boy, however, I saw firsthand two outstanding examples of impeccable integrity that impressed me greatly. I also saw two other truly great examples of integrity while I was in the real estate business.

My father worked on a railroad. When someone had worked for that company for ten years, the employee was given what they called an annual pass. With the pass he and his family members were entitled to ride all passenger trains free of charge. When my father had worked for the company only nine years he received by mail an annual pass. The company had made a mistake.

Even though I was only nine or ten years of age, I had been taught that dishonesty was wrong. I thought the only thing for him to do was send it back. My father discussed it briefly with my mother and returned the pass to the company. I was deeply impressed.

My uncle, who was terribly poor, eked out a living on a small hillside farm. He bought a huge cow with intention of selling it from a man who was old and also terribly poor. The owner of the cow had no idea how much the cow was worth. Coming back from the market after selling the cow, my uncle told me he had to take some more money to the man from whom he had bought it.

I asked him if he had paid the man what the man had asked for the cow. My uncle said he had, but the man was old and had no idea what the cow was worth. Therefore, according to my uncle, since he had made a large profit from the sale of the cow, the man he had bought the cow from deserved more money. My uncle, true to his word, paid the man more money. Again I was deeply impressed.

As a real estate broker I attempted to sell a house for a client. My contract with him designated a ninety-day period in which I had to sell the property. If I sold it I would be paid a commission of five percent of the selling price. I put forth my best effort and advertised it sufficiently, but I did not sell it.

Two or three months after the expiration of my contract with the owner of the property, I received a check from him for the full amount of what the commission would have been had I sold the property. I called him and asked what the check was for. He said, "It was the commission for the sale of the house." I told him he didn't owe me anything because I had not sold the property. He said that, in his opinion, the property had sold because of the way I had exposed it to the market and that it was only fair to pay me.

A fellow real estate broker called my office wanting to know whether we had any houses for sale in a certain area. We told him of three or four. He called back and informed us that he had sold one of them. I asked him which one. He said, "The Bradshaw house." I told him that our contract with that homeowner had expired and that he did not owe us any part of the commission. He said, "No, I saw one of your For Sale signs leaning against a fence at the side of the lot. I talked to the owner and found that it was still for sale. Your sign was the reason we made the sale. Therefore, you are entitled to half the commission."

These four people demonstrated impeccable integrity. No law or custom required them to do the things they did. They would not have been criticized or blamed had they not paid out what they had.

However, they undoubtedly would have felt uncomfortable not living according to what they believed. They therefore elected to absolve themselves and have the suffrage of the world. An additional benefit of following their conscience was that others who knew about their integrity would want to do business with them and would recommend them to their neighbors and friends. The world, in effect, would vote for them.

An ounce of loyalty is worth a pound of cleverness.

Elbert Hubbard

Selling automobiles as a young man was a needed experience for me. Herbert Daniels (not his real name), the Chevrolet dealer for whom I worked, was truly a man of enormous loyalty and integrity. He was totally loyal in all situations. As an employee he was loyal to his employer. He managed the parts department and did a quality job. The business was owned jointly by a man and his wife. The husband who managed the business suddenly passed away, leaving his widow with that tremendous responsibility.

As it was told to me, since she knew nothing about managing a business and since Daniels had been so loyal as manager of the parts department, she made him acting manager of the business. A short time later she sold him 51 percent of the business with the understanding that he could pay for it from future profits.

As an employer he was loyal to his employees. He was loyal to his customers and also to the policies of the factory that furnished the dealership the cars it sold.

In order to be loyal in all situations, one needs to be a man of impeccable integrity. When he hired me he told me that if he ever found out that I had lied to one of his customers, he would fire me. He said, "If you lie to them, you will lie to me."

He wanted every customer of his to get exactly what he thought he was getting. In those days rolling the odometer back on a used car with high mileage was a common practice. This made it appear to be a car that had not been driven so much. Daniels did not allow that to be done on the cars his company sold. He would have fired anyone for doing it.

The company had an appraiser who placed a value on the cars we took in trade. He went over each trade-in meticulously to determine what it would cost to return it to good condition. He subtracted that figure from the book value of the car. The figure at which he arrived was rounded off to a reasonable figure. That was the value placed on the car.

The figure the appraiser came up with was the amount the salesmen were allowed to present for the car. We were never allowed to deviate from that figure. That was the price that was placed on the trade-in. There was never any dickering or bargaining until a car had been around for thirty days. Then the company continued to lower the price until the car was sold. What's more, we always sold each new car for the exact factory recommended price. Every customer received the exact same treatment.

The used cars that were esteemed to be in good condition both mechanically and in appearance were sold with a thirty-day warranty. Anything the purchaser wanted to have done during that thirty-day period would be done by the company for half price. If something needed to be repaired and had been missed, which happened occasionally, the company took care of it free of charge.

We salesmen were paid straight commission, which was a certain percent of the sales price of the car. Most automobile salesmen in those days were paid this way. There was no salary or guaranteed income. Our dealer always paid his salesmen 25 percent more than the rate paid by most other dealers.

When automobile manufacturers ceased to manufacture cars because of World War II, there were no cars available and would not be for years. Daniels advised his customers to place an order for a new car. He knew when they became available there would be a huge pent-up demand for new cars. Many of his customers did just that. It was late in 1941 when they ceased to build new cars for domestic use.

There were no new cars available for the market until 1946 or 1947. When they became available, Daniels, the dealer, sold them at the factory recommended price that was less than half the amount for which he could have sold them because the demand was so great.

When the car that I had ordered came in, a 1947 Chevrolet sedan, he sold it to me for a little more than $1,100. I went directly from the dealership where I took delivery of the car to a barbershop, where I parked right at the front door. As I walked in the shop, the owner of the shop said, "I don't care what you paid for that car; I will give you twice what you paid."

I asked Daniels why he was selling the cars for

so much less than he could get for them. His reply was, "These are my customers. I do not want to gouge them. I want their business when cars here become plentiful again."

Here was a very, very wise and prudent man, a man that lived strictly by the dictates of his conscience. He seemed to have reaped much more than he had sown. He retired at a fairly young age with sufficient resources to live the kind of a life he wanted to live, doing the things he wanted to do.

What Herbert Daniels did was not strenuous. It was not difficult to do. It was something everyone can easily do. This method of doing business always results in success. When the word gets out, people will come in droves to do business with you. This will give you a happy life plus tremendous financial rewards.

No man need live a minute longer as he is, because the creator endowed him with the ability to change himself.

J.C. Penney

If you are a cigarette smoker, you do not need to live a minute longer as you are if you do not want to. The Creator endowed you with the ability to quit smoking at any minute. You can easily, with no ill effects, no misery, and no lingering craving, kick the cigarette habit out of your life forever.

Mark Twain said, "It is easy to quit. I have quit a thousand times." Mark Twain was right. It is easy to quit. I may have broken his record. I have quit many, many times: for an hour, two hours, a day, three days, a week, and many times for even longer periods. I quit once for more than a year.

My problem was I did not quit craving cigarettes. I simply could not tolerate the terrible agony, the utter misery of doing without that nicotine, and would decide to smoke *just one* more. Of course, if you are a smoker and have tried to quit, you know that did not work.

I smoked for forty-four years. As soon as I realized I was hooked, I began trying to quit. I tried every method, every technique and every concoction I had ever heard of, all to no avail. I simply could not lay them down.

While puffing on a cigarette one day, I happened to begin a conversation with an elderly neighbor who was a retired medical doctor. He mentioned that he would be derelict in his duty if he did not warn me of the dangers of smoking. I told him I could not quit. He proceeded to tell me how I could kick the habit without having to go through a lot of misery. He said, "There will be no discomfort, no misery, and no lingering craving."

I was severely addicted, had tried so desperately to quit, but the craving was always so intense that I could not accept what he said about not having this craving. I did not think anything as simple as the method he recommended would be effective in my case, so for many years I ignored his advice.

As the years went by, though, I became increasingly concerned about how smoking was probably damaging my health. Since nothing else I had attempted had helped me to quit, I finally decided to try what the doctor had suggested.

What the doctor recommended involves the

awesome power of the imagination. He recommended that just as I was about to drop off to sleep each night that I imagine myself as a nonsmoker. He said to imagine, every night, someone offering me a cigarette and me telling them, "No, thank you. I don't smoke." Additionally, he said to imagine some friend asking me if I had a cigarette I could let him have and me telling him, "No, I don't smoke. Therefore I never carry them." He recommended that I go through the same process each morning just as I awakened from my sleep. He also recommended that I imagine myself being thankful and happy to be a nonsmoker.

I was not aware of it at the time, but because of the power of the imagination, this technique was virtually bound to succeed. Dr Alex F. Osborne, in his book *Psychocybernetics*, said, "The creative power of the imagination is all but limitless." Wallace Stevens put it a bit differently, but it amounts to the same thing: "We say God and the imagination are one."

I was somewhat doubtful that the technique would work, but I decided to give the program a try and to follow it faithfully. I did not tell anyone of my plan. My thinking was that if I told anyone, I would then be under pressure to make it happen. I did not want that pressure. I did not check to see whether the craving was diminishing. I just continued to smoke and to enjoy it as usual.

As I was driving along after four or five weeks of this, I reached for a cigarette. I started to light it, but to my great amazement I realized I did not want it. I rechecked myself. No, I did not want it at all. The desire was gone, the habit broken. The addiction, the craving, was gone. Thirty-six years have passed since then, and to this day I have not had the slightest desire to smoke.

You can quit. This method of quitting will work for you and free you from the habit. You will be so thankful, and you will like yourself so much more, be so much healthier and happier, that you will wonder, like I did, why you couldn't have discovered this method long before. You, your clothes, your hair, your car and your home will no longer stink. You will have more money to spend for things you want. Ridding yourself of the habit will add life to your years, and in all probability it will also add years to your life.

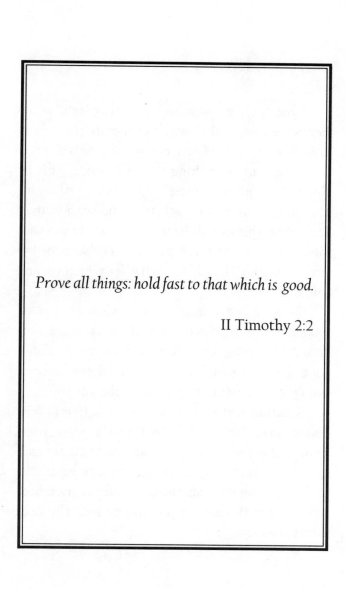

Prove all things: hold fast to that which is good.

II Timothy 2:2

One of the greatest and most wonderful privileges we have is that we can generate the belief, confidence or faith to be, to do, or to have anything and everything that we desire. This is done by programming ourselves with our thinking, with positive self-talk, and with visualizing how things will be when we are in possession of the object of our desire. It is also done by pretending we already have that for which we are longing.

Quoting four stanzas of Longfellow's poem "A Psalm of Life" repeatedly, which was tantamount to self-talk, programmed me to accomplish a life-long desire: to find work where dress clothes would be appropriate to wear on the job.

Reading and rereading the book *How to Win Friends and Influence People,* by Dale Carnegie, programmed me to leave my job as a meat cutter and get back into selling. Constantly thinking about and searching for something to sell programmed me to leave the bakery job and go into the real estate business.

PROGRAM YOURSELF FOR SUCCESS

Positive self-talk, over a long period of time, programmed me to accomplish an apparently impossible task. That task was starting another real estate business with less than $100.00.

I programmed myself for each of these accomplishments but I did not think of either of them as programming myself. I was not aware that such a thing was possible.

I quoted the poem because I liked what it said. I read and reread Carnegie's book because of what it was teaching me. I was so intensely interested in finding a product to sell that was plentiful and where deliveries would present no problem, I programmed myself to go into the real estate business in Logan by thinking about it constantly. I used positive self-talk to program myself to go into the business in Huntington because the book *The Magic of Believing,* by Claude M. Bristol, recommended it.

I had accomplished all these things by programming myself when I had no idea such a thing was possible. Programming was not something people talked about in those days.

I mentioned earlier that at the age of eighty-eight I was the conductor of a radio show. I decided to put the idea of programming oneself to an authentic test. To do that I would have to intentionally program myself to accomplish a goal that would appear to be impossible.

I used every programming technique of which I was aware. Remembering what an impact listening to those records had had on my son, Ben Jr., I decided to try that route. I thought listening to a series of recorded positive assertions would be a good way for me to program myself.

I wrote a short speech telling myself that I could do it. I told myself the need was great, that the way was open and I only needed to find it. I do not remember all that I wrote. But it was about a five-minute speech, which I recorded repeatedly on both sides of a thirty-minute cassette tape.

I put the tape in the tape player in my car. Every time I turned my ignition on, the tape started telling me I could do it. I also practiced what William James recommended: "Act in cold blood as if the thing in question were real, and it will become infallibly real." I pretended it was real by doing as I had done when I programmed myself to conduct seminars. Every time I got in my car to go anywhere I pretended to be going to a radio station to put my program on the air. Every time I came home I pretended to be coming home from the radio station.

This continued for four or five weeks. Then I got a hunch that I should go to a small city about twenty-five miles away. I knew from the beginning that I did not want be on a local station, and I also knew that I did not want to pay for the radio time. I knew very little about the town because I had been there only a few times.

As I drove down the main street, I saw four big letters near the top of a two-story building. I knew it was a radio station. There was a vacant parking space right in front of the entrance to the building. I parked and went up some stairs to the second floor, where I met a man in a hall. He said, "Can I help you?" I told him I wanted to talk to someone about some radio time.

He introduced me to a woman who was the manager of the station. She asked me the same question, "Can I help you?" I gave her the same answer. She asked me if I was a minister. I told her

I was not. She then asked me what I was going to talk about. I told her I wanted to tell people how to use more of what they were born with in order to be more successful. She wanted to know what I was going to call my program. After thinking about it a moment, I told her "The Old Philosopher."

After a brief discussion the man said, "Oh, hell, put him on next Wednesday at 12:30, right after the news." I then asked what this was going to cost me. The man said, "There will be no charge."

I put my show on the next Wednesday. Everyone at the station thought it was good and said they were looking forward to hearing me the next week. I continued that for, I think, sixteen weeks. Then a terrible storm put the station off the air for several days. During that period I was not able to put the show on the air. I therefore decided to end my radio career.

I had proven, though, that you can definitely program yourself to achieve anything, no matter how difficult it seems, and you can definitely experience precisely that which you had programmed yourself to experience.

PROGRAM YOURSELF FOR SUCCESS

Every success story related in this book revolves around programming. As I mentioned much earlier in this book, when I was a young man I began programming myself, even though I did not use the term "programming." Each person I have discussed in this book, whether or not they thought of it in these terms, programmed himself or herself for success. This programming technique will work for you, as well. Think about it: if there are changes you would like to bring about in your life, why not give these programming techniques a try?

Some statements in this book need to be reiterated. Keep them with you.

"Everyone is born with a special talent."

You are perfectly equipped to become, to do and to have all the things, conditions, situations and circumstances you most want in life.

Your mind is as fertile, as creative and as capable as any mind that ever existed in mortal man.

B. F. Skinner theorized that the things human beings and animals do, they do because they are mentally conditioned to do them.

"Every act of man springs from the hidden seed of thought and could not have appeared without them. The outer world of circumstance shapes itself to the inner world of thought. All that a man achieves and all that he fails to achieve is the direct result of his own thought.

"The self-image is a golden key to living a better life because of two important discoveries."

All your actions, feelings, behavior—even your abilities—are always consistent with this self-image. In short, you "will act" like the sort of person you conceive yourself to be.

Not only this, but you literally cannot act otherwise, in spite of all your conscious effort or willpower. The man who conceives himself to be a "failure-type person" will find a way to fail, in spite of all his good intentions or willpower, even if opportunity is literally dumped in his lap.

The self-image can be changed; numerous case histories have shown that no one is ever too young or too old to change his self-image and thereby start to live a new life....

"Whatever is maintained as an image in the mind will make its way into the outer world and manifest itself as a physical fact."

The only way one can achieve any goal is to program oneself to achieve it.

When one is thoroughly programmed to achieve a goal, he is totally confident he will achieve it. He will act without fear or concern.

Acknowledgements

The author would like to thank all of his family members for their encouragement and support; as well as Margaret (Margo) Smith, Chris Washington, and Patrick Grace.

Reflections

_____

_____

_____

_____

_____

_____

_____

_____

_____

_____

_____

_____

_____

_____

_____

_____

_____

_____

_____

_____

_____

_____

_____

_____

_____

_____

_____

_____

_____

_____

_____

_____

_____

_____

_____